Improving Competitive Advantage

Chartered Management Institute Open Learning Programme

OTHER BOOKS WITHIN THIS SERIES

Using Information for Decision-Making	0750664274
Developing Personal Potential	0750664231
Creating a Customer Focus	0750664266
Maximizing Resources	075066424X
The Performance Manager	0750664215
Successful Project Management	0750664193
Developing High Performance Teams	0750664207
Communication in Organizations	0750664282
Positive Recruitment and Retention	0750664223

IMPROVING COMPETITIVE ADVANTAGE

Second edition

Revised by: Corinne Leech

Series Editor: Kate Williams

chartered
management
institute

AMSTERDAM • BOSTON • HEIDELBERG • LONDON • OXFORD • NEW YORK • PARIS • SAN DIEGO • SAN FRANCISCO • SINGAPORE • SYDNEY • TOKYO

Elsevier
Linacre House, Jordan Hill, Oxford OX2 8DP
200 Wheeler Road, Burlington, MA 01803

First published 1997
Second edition 2004

British Library Cataloguing in Publication Data
A catalogue record for this book is available from the British Library

ISBN 0 7506 6425 8

For information on all Elsevier publications visit our website at http://books.elsevier.com

Revised by: Corinne Leech
Editor: Kate Williams
Based on previous material in the Chartered Management Institute Opening Learning Programme, 1997. Series Editor: Gareth Lewis.

Typeset by Charon Tec Pvt. Ltd, Chennai, India
Printed and bound in Italy

Contents

Series overview

The Chartered Management Institute Flexible Learning Programme is a series of workbooks prepared by the Chartered Management Institute and Elsevier for managers seeking to develop themselves.

Comprising ten open learning workbooks, the programme covers the best of modern management theory and practice. Each workbook provides a range of frameworks and techniques to improve your effectiveness as a manager, thus helping you acquire the knowledge and skill to make you fully competent in your role.

Each workbook is written by an experienced management writer and covers an important management topic or theme. The activities both reinforce learning and help to relate the generic ideas to your individual work context. While coverage of each topic is fully comprehensive, additional reading suggestions and reference sources are given for those who wish to study to a greater depth.

Designed to be practical, stimulating and challenging, the aim of the workbooks is to improve performance at work by benefiting you and your organization. This practical focus is at the heart of the competence-based approach that has been adopted by the programme.

Introduction

Most managers know quite well that management by 'Flavour of the month' is never a good idea. If the Holy Grail of management existed, it would have been found by now. There is no universal panacea but common sense dictates that any organization has to deliver services and products which attract and then satisfy their customers.

By focusing on customer expectations, and analysing the external and internal environments, organizations need to define exactly:

- What should be offered to the customer
- At what price
- What distribution channels will be used
- How the customer will get to know about it (i.e. how will it be promoted)
- What the customer will experience when they make contact with the organization.

But in order to make the offering to the customer a reality the organization has to have the right:

- People to do the work
- Processes to enable the people to deliver.

This workbook focuses on improving competitive advantage through people and processes. It explores the concept of total quality management (TQM) and looks at the practicalities of continually striving to improve processes through empowering people.

Objectives

By the end of the workbook you will be better able to:

- identify the underlying principles of implementing quality management in the workplace
- review your techniques for involving your team in improving the quality of the team's output
- identify your team processes and what they contribute to the organization
- document existing processes using process mapping techniques
- identify the relevant people to assist in the process mapping process
- use process mapping to improve processes
- identify quality checkpoints along your team's processes and select appropriate measures
- benchmark processes against similar processes elsewhere in the organization or in external organizations
- use techniques which will help team members to accept change and improve performance
- implement health and safety legal requirements.

Section 1 Introducing quality

Introduction

This section of the workbook gives you an overview of total quality management (TQM) and the philosophy of continually striving to make improvements. It introduces the two main strands of the TQM approach: process management and human resource management. These two strands are explored in detail in later sections of the workbook.

TQM is based on solid, balanced management principles. Even though your organization may not be implementing a TQM system (such as ISO 9000/2000 or the EFQM Excellence Model), the philosophy behind TQM is valuable for any team to incorporate.

What is quality?

What do you understand by the term 'quality'? Formulating a definition that works for every organization can be tricky. What do a small hairdressing salon, a major university, a cinema and an electricity-generating plant have in common? They all have **customers**.

One of the most important developments in the evolution of quality thinking from its beginnings in the 1920s to the present, is that quality is primarily defined not in terms of adherence to a specification, but in terms of what the customer wants (Figure 1.1).

As the chief executive of one total quality organization put it, 'Quality is what our customers say it is'. This healthy shift of focus has allowed the application of quality concepts from manufacturing to a much wider range of organizations (including service organizations and public sector organizations) and a much wider range of activities (including administrative and managerial activities). In public service organizations, the concept of stakeholders is often substituted for the idea of customers, but, in general, the effect is the same.

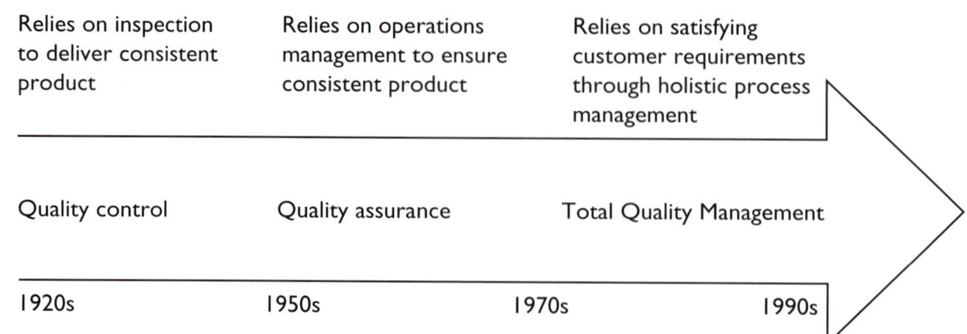

Figure 1.1 The evolution of quality concepts

H. J. Harrington, a leading American quality analyst, suggests that quality should be defined as:

Meeting or exceeding customer expectations, at a price that represents value for money to them, and delivering your product or service when they need it.

(Harrington, p. 40)[1]

Customers' expectations include not only the features of the products or services they buy, but all-important aspects of customer service such as courtesy and product knowledge as well. These intangible elements are encompassed in the pithiest definition of quality:

Quality is delighting the customer.

WHAT DOES QUALITY MEAN TO AN ORGANIZATION?

There are a number of advantages to pursuing quality as a business strategy. In the present complex and rapidly changing environment, customers tend to be sophisticated and demanding. As Allen Paison, President of Walker Customer Satisfaction Measurement commented:

'Customers today want quality and value in the products and services they buy. Moreover, they usually can find it, and tend to look until they do.'

Organizations that fail to deliver quality are on the road to extinction. Organizations that compete on quality rather than price can avoid the business suicide caused by destructive price wars. Running high-quality systems internally ensures cost-effective operations which maximize profits and allow efficiency savings to be passed along to customers. In the UK and the rest of Europe, total quality initiatives have been used to streamline operations, increase productivity, cut costs and expand market share. Quality means:

- survival
- competitiveness
- success.

The principles of TQM

A number of management experts have contributed to the concepts and philosophy of TQM, and the ideas of the most important gurus are outlined in Appendix A. For now, we will examine the most important principles of TQM in overview.

PUT THE CUSTOMER FIRST

This is the golden rule of the total quality approach. It involves thinking like a customer: finding out what customers want, putting their needs and desires first, and thinking backwards through the organization's systems to ensure excellence of delivery.

Customers can be internal or external

A customer can be defined as the recipient of an output or activity. Of course this includes external customers who purchase a product or service. It also includes internal customers, the people inside the organization who are the next link in the process chain. This means that everyone in the organization is linked in supplier–customer relationships, with all the responsibilities for customer satisfaction that this entails.

Examples of internal customers include people who use the reprographics department, or warehouse packers who receive customer orders from the sales department. The reprographics customers need copies to be legible, with the pages in the right order, and securely stapled. The warehouse packers – the customers of the sales department – need order forms to be legible and accurate, and to include complete information such as the customer's post code. If these quality requirements are not met, it causes the internal customer problems, frustration, and time and increases the organization's costs.

ACTIVITY 1

Who are the customers for your outputs at work? Try to identify three types of internal customers, for the various types of outputs you are responsible for in your organization.

1

2

3

Looking at organizational activities in terms of internal customers can be surprisingly revolutionary in that it tends to subvert the familiar patterns of both organizational hierarchy and functional divisions. In other words it cuts across organizational structure both vertically and horizontally (Figure 1.2).

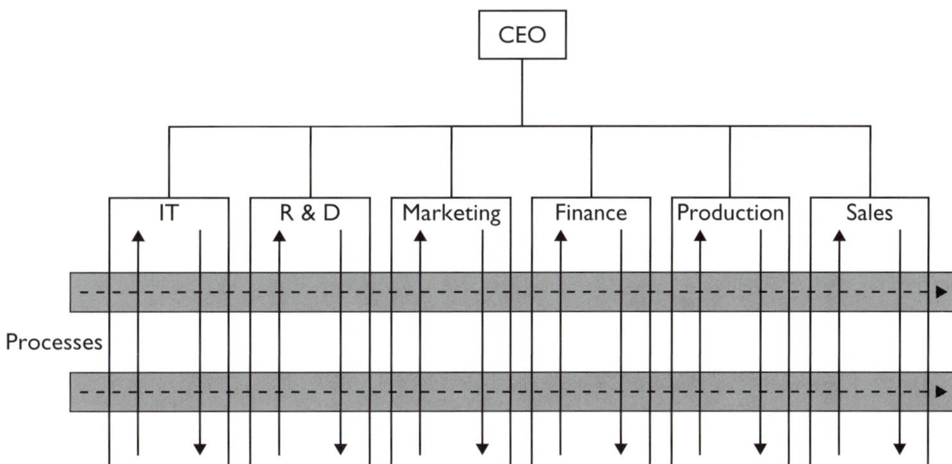

Figure 1.2 Relationships between internal suppliers and customers can cut across both vertical and horizontal boundaries

For example, one internal customer of a senior manager may be his or her secretary who has a legitimate cause for complaint if the manager produces indecipherable handwriting to process. This would be an example of the supplier–customer relationship cutting across vertical levels of an organization's hierarchy.

Customer–supplier relationships can also cross functional (horizontal) boundaries. An example of this would be when the finance department receives financial information from a number of different budget-holding centres during its annual budget preparation. In this case, the finance department is the customer and the budget centres are the suppliers.

Organizations are customers too

An important element of the customer-first approach is that the organization also needs to become a more demanding customer. External suppliers are vitally important to the smoothness and quality of an organization's processes. An organization pursuing total quality cannot afford bought-in supplies, components, or services being substandard. Such organizations often renegotiate their relationship with external suppliers, working with and accrediting a small number of excellent, reliable suppliers. With such suppliers, customer organizations tend to develop close, co-operative relationships, which often includes elements such as:

- advice and assistance in specifying standards and designing processes
- joint training initiatives
- just-in-time delivery.

ACTIVITIES AS PROCESSES

Systems theory, developed in the 1960s, allows any activity to be analysed as a process, which takes in inputs, acts on them, and delivers outputs. This model (Figure 1.3) can apply to any process, from the simplest, such as ringing up a purchase on a till, to the most complex, such as launching a rocket into space. (Complex processes are made up of a number of interlocking subprocesses.)

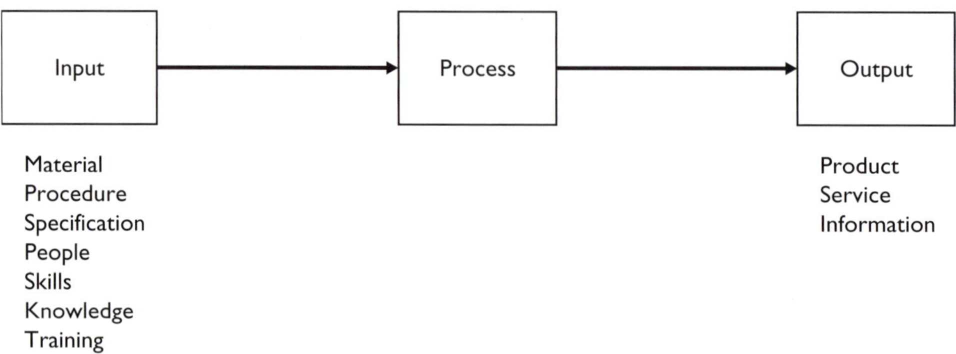

Figure 1.3 The process model

The advantage of viewing organizational activities as processes is that processes can be analysed, measured, managed, and improved. We look at this in detail in later sections of the workbook.

QUALITY IS FREE

This maxim, from quality guru Philip Crosby, can seem both contentious and confusing. Certainly quality is not free if you don't already have it. For example, introducing and running a total quality initiative is not free. Cost effective, yes; providing excellent value for money and return on investment, yes. Free, no.

Crosby's point is easier to understand if we turn his statement on its head, and say that lack of quality is expensive. Compared to the costs of poor quality – which include loss of market share and higher operating costs – maintaining quality systems is free. Once they are up and running, systems and operations producing defect-free, high-quality output, are, in effect, providing quality for free.

PREVENTION IS BETTER THAN CURE ...

... and much, much cheaper. Quality costs, or more accurately, poor-quality costs, fall into three general areas:

- Prevention costs, which include resources spent on ensuring that deviations from quality don't occur.
- Appraisal costs, which include the costs of inspecting both suppliers' materials and the organization's own output to ensure conformity to specification.
- Failure costs, including the costs of scrap, reworking, handling customer complaints, warranties, servicing, replacements and refunds.

Of these costs, prevention costs are by far the lowest. For example, it costs five times less to retain a satisfied customer (i.e. to prevent a customer defection) than to find a new customer. The further a mistake travels toward the final, external customer, the greater its costs escalate (see Figure 1.4).

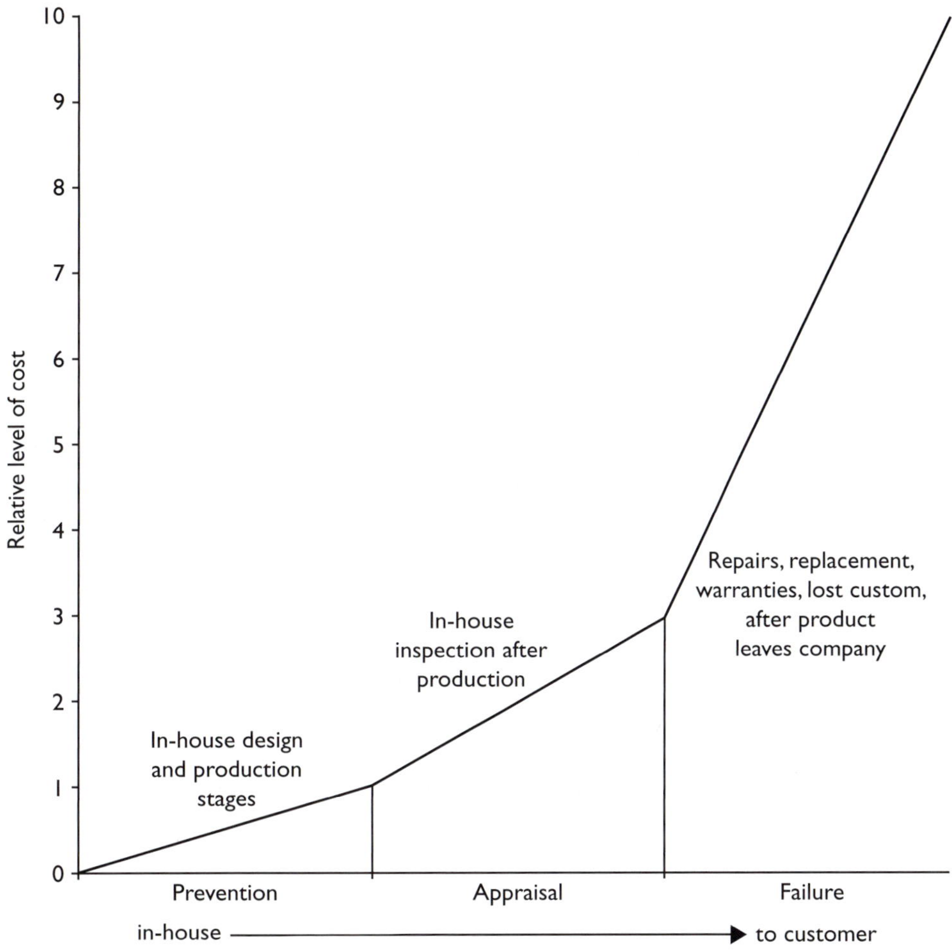

Figure 1.4 Relative values of prevention, appraisal, and failure costs

The cost to organizations of having poor quality has been estimated at between 15 and 40 per cent of turnover. These costs can be slashed by introducing a quality initiative. According to Harrington, 'It is reasonable to expect poor-quality cost to be cut 30 per cent over a 3-year period after the improvement process is fully implemented.'[1]

ACTIVITY 2

Do you know how much poor-quality costs your department each year?

REDUCE VARIATION AND AIM FOR ZERO DEFECTS

Deviation from quality is the result of variation from a required standard or specification. In a technical sense, improving quality is a matter of reducing variation. Systems should be designed – and employees trained and empowered – to deliver a performance level of 'zero defects' (another of Crosby's terms). While attaining absolute perfection is unlikely, it is important to aim for it, as this is most likely to enable the organization to achieve the highest quality possible.

QUALITY IS EVERYONE'S RESPONSIBILITY

For total quality to work, it must be embedded at the heart of the organization. This means making employees at all levels accountable for the quality of their work. It also means creating working conditions which give them the power to achieve quality; for example, giving assembly line workers the authority to reject a substandard part or to stop production lines if variations reach a certain critical level. Quality initiatives should enable the organization to tap the creativity and experience of every employee.

The total quality approach poses particular challenges to managers, because it requires them to consult and listen to employees, act on the problems they identify, and devolve authority to them. Total quality often demands a cultural change in the organization, in which managers must redefine their roles and use a more participative, empowering management style. Total quality initiatives will be unsuccessful unless one of their goals is to produce a significant improvement in the quality of employees' working lives.

ACTIVITY 3

How many of the principles of TQM are consciously promoted and followed in your organization at the moment?

In the following table, identify evidence which demonstrates the importance of each principle to your organization. Evaluate the evidence for the level of commitment to the principle that it illustrates. In the rating column:

- write 0 if there is no evidence relating the principle to the organization
- write 1 if the evidence demonstrates an awareness of the principle
- write 2 if the evidence demonstrates unofficial, piecemeal efforts to implement the principle
- write 3 if the evidence demonstrates systematic, organization-wide procedures and processes designed to put the principle into practice.

Principle	**Evidence of importance in my organization**	**Rating**
Putting the customer first		
Seeing activities as processes		
Reducing poor-quality costs		
Reducing variation		
Preventing, not rectifying, mistakes		
Making quality everyone's responsibility		

Quality management: how it succeeds, why it fails

THE RISKS AND REWARDS

Quality management is not a low-risk strategy. Managers of organizations considering adopting a quality approach need to carefully weigh up the possible risks and rewards, to decide whether it is right for them.

The advantages of a successful quality initiative include:

- satisfied or delighted customers
- high morale among employees at all levels: job satisfaction, pride and enjoyment
- improved relationships with suppliers
- increased productivity
- reductions in poor-quality costs
- retaining or extending market share
- the ability to attract and retain high-quality employees
- the optimization of resources including the creativity and loyalty of employees.

The disadvantages of a quality initiative can include:

- cost: instituting a quality initiative requires investment, which may not begin to show returns for 2 to 3 years
- time: instituting a successful quality initiative requires up to 2 years
- short to medium term decreases in productivity; during implementation, employees at all levels will spend significant time away from their ordinary jobs in order to focus on their part of the quality initiative
- its requirement for emotional energy, commitment, faith and trust
- its potential to create bureaucracy and increase paperwork
- the 'burnt bridges' factor: there is no going back to old habits or procedures
- the risk that a failed initiative can seriously damage morale.

CONDITIONS THAT FOSTER SUCCESS

In the 1980s, Tom Peters estimated that up to 98 per cent of quality initiatives fail. Fortunately, experience of quality programmes during the last decade in the UK (and even longer in the US) has led experts and practitioners to a number of conclusions about why such initiatives succeed or fail. Nowadays, organizations launching a quality initiative have a greater chance of success if they are willing to learn from other organizations' mistakes and triumphs.

Three important factors which make for success have been identified:

- organizational culture
- leadership and management style
- organizational ability to consolidate and apply new learning.

Organizational culture is a critical issue for successful quality programmes. Organizations which already have a favourable culture will find that the implementation of a quality initiative progresses more smoothly. Organizations that do not have a favourable culture will have a rougher ride, but can still be successful if they act on the understanding that fundamentally changing the culture is an essential, perhaps *the* essential, prerequisite for success.

A favourable organizational culture is one in which there is a reasonable degree of trust and communication:

- among managers
- between management and the workforce.

Morale is high. Departmental fortresses have not been allowed to flourish and create suspicion, jealousy or hostility between functional divisions. Generally such organizations have a progressive, best-practice attitude to human resource management and development.

In short, the organization has already absorbed and put into practice a number of the 'soft' skills on which quality management draws so heavily. Good foundations are already in place for further advances in the areas of staff consultation, teamwork, and two-way communication both horizontally, between departments, and vertically, between the hierarchical levels of the organization.

One vital influence on culture is leadership and management style. Successful quality initiatives tend to have 'forthright but listening' leaders.[2] Their management style tends to be participative rather than autocratic or authoritarian. The most fortunate organizations have the benefit of transformational leaders, who can inspire or provoke change rather than impose it. Such leaders make it clear that, while attaining quality is a non-negotiable goal, the journey to quality is a collective adventure for the organization. They generate excitement about the change programme, and involve all levels of the organization in defining and pursuing quality. In this way, quality is integrated into the heart of the organization, rather than remaining a faddish add on.

The final success factor relates to the ability of the organization to become a 'learning organization'. There are two aspects to this issue:

- creating a learning environment
- consolidating gains.

Establishing a learning environment involves creating a climate where employees are allowed to learn by doing, where theoretical training is always tied into working practice. Research confirms that people learn best when they feel safe. Employees must be allowed time for learning by experimentation, in a safe atmosphere where risk taking is encouraged and failure is accepted without blame or ridicule. This is the best environment for encouraging creativity and innovation and the one most likely to produce substantive quality improvements.

Innovation and learning are unlikely to result in bottom-line gains, however, unless the organization has a relentless commitment to apply and integrate them into every part of the organization that could benefit. For example, it is no good for the information technology (IT) department to develop a powerful database system which the marketing and sales departments cannot be persuaded to use. Quality improvements must be driven by the commitment to find practical, workable applications and implement them as widely as possible across the organization.

The following activity helps you to consolidate your learning in this section.

ACTIVITY 4

1 Give a working definition of quality which could be applied to virtually any organization.

2 Explain the term 'process chain'.

3 What are the implications of putting the customer first? List three or four.

4 What is an internal customer?

5 Why is prevention better than cure, in quality terms?

6 Explain the terms 'reducing variation' and 'zero defects'.

7 What are the two major elements involved in running a successful quality programme?

FEEDBACK

If you had difficulties with any question in the previous activity, refresh your memory by re-reading the relevant section. Or you might find it useful to discuss the issue with a colleague.

Learning summary

- The focus of a quality management approach is pleasing the customer. Thus, quality may be defined as satisfying or surpassing customer expectations. Pursuing quality as a business strategy has a number of potential advantages, including expanding market share, cutting costs and increasing customer and employee satisfaction.
- Quality management depends on putting into practice several important principles. Pleasing customers – whether external or internal – becomes the primary focus of the organization's efforts. Quality must become the responsibility of everyone in the organization.
- Activities are managed as processes, having inputs, actions and outputs; this allows them to be measured, analysed and improved. The lack of quality, in terms of defects, errors and inefficiencies, is costly to an organization. The most efficient way of reducing poor-quality costs is to prevent, rather than rectify, defects (understood as variations from quality standards).
- Managing quality depends on the effective use of two separate but interdependent sets of skills. 'Hard' or technical skills, are employed to analyse processes, solve problems, and generate and evaluate improvements. 'Soft' or people management skills are used to gain commitment and input from employees at every level of the organization. Without the competent use of both types of skills, quality initiatives can fail.

- A quality initiative tends to be most successful if the organization either already has, or makes a top priority of creating, a culture in which trust, healthy morale and participative, democratic styles of management, predominate. Good human resource management is also a key factor. 'Learning organizations', which capitalize on improvements and rigorously apply them to every possible area of the organization, also tend to succeed.

References

1 Adapted from *The Improvement Process*, by H. J. Harrington (1987), p. 40.
2 *Managing Change*, by Philip Sadler, Kogan Page (1995).

Section 2 People and quality

Introduction

People management skills are one strand of the two-pronged approach needed to achieve quality. Quality depends on everyone in the organization pulling together. If employees are not properly motivated, this simply will not happen.

In this section of the workbook you will find some of the people management skills needed to make quality work. These skills include the interpersonal and human resource management skills of:

- empowering employees to take responsibility for quality in their own work
- identifying and providing the training necessary to achieve this
- organizing and running quality improvement groups in teams.

You will need to refer to other workbooks in the series, such as *Developing High Performance Teams* and *The Performance Manager,* for a detailed exploration of people management skills.

Quality is everyone's responsibility

As you saw in Section 1, one of the major principles of quality management is that process chains extend beyond the functional departments and divisions of traditional organizational structures. To improve processes, an organization must pay careful attention to the hand-over points where work moves from one team or department to another (i.e. from an internal supplier to an internal customer).

Quality is incremental. Many small improvements can result in large-scale quality increases and the substantial bottom-line gains which accompany them. The steady flow of incremental improvements will dry up, however, without the active participation of each member of a team. Everyone must be involved in the push for quality, or potential improvements will fall through the cracks. Everyone must feel responsible to their internal as well as their external customers, or internal waste will multiply and the organization will be unable to provide affordable quality to the final customer.

Any team must have a common view of quality which all team members understand and share. The organization must also make the necessary structural and procedural changes so that:

- communication can flow upwards from operational teams to senior management
- employees have the authority to make decisions concerning quality in their own work.

Only if this happens can incremental improvements become established and start to build up quality and pare down poor-quality costs.

ACTIVITY 5

1 Are there areas in your department where quality suffers because employees are not allowed to take responsibility for their work?

2 Do you feel you are sufficiently in touch with your team to give an accurate answer to this question?

FEEDBACK

As Peter Drucker has said, 'The individual worker knows better than anyone else what makes him or her effective. The only true expert is the person who does the job'. Quality initiatives seek to tap into – and benefit from – this pool of expertise. The necessary changes that promote this include:

- measuring processes, not people (e.g. Deming[1] advocates eliminating numerical targets for employees)
- removing barriers to communication, including management's tendency to talk but not listen
- recognizing that employees want to do a good job
- instigating measures that promote employee empowerment.

Empowerment

Empowerment is a management method which involves team members participating in, or controlling aspects of, work that was traditionally the preserve of management. Empowerment means sharing responsibility, information, and a higher level of decision-making with your team. Empowerment entails a greater degree of transparency and communication in the decision-making process. Management and teams share information, and managers tend to consult with employees before making a decision, and to explain their decisions to them afterwards. In this sense, empowerment requires participatory leadership.

Routine decisions are handed over to team members. For example, team members would monitor their own work and have the authority to take action if they spot a quality problem.

Empowered organizations tend to have flatter management structures and to emphasize teamwork. The roles of supervisors and front-line managers shift from that of 'inspector' to that of 'team facilitator'. Teams are taught the techniques of problem solving and effective group working, and are expected to use them and to take responsibility for achieving and maintaining quality. Procedures become more flexible and less rule-bound as front-line staff are given more discretion. In empowered organizations, employees 'own' both the successes and the problems arising from their work.

Increasing team members' levels of responsibility will not be effective, however, if they are afraid of being punished for mistakes. Empowerment must take place in tandem with cultural changes which remove any traces of a 'blame culture'.

Your style of management is likely to have the greatest impact on how empowered your team members feel.

ACTIVITY 6

Give three examples of things that contribute towards members of your team feeling empowered.

FEEDBACK

Practical strategies to contribute towards a feeling of empowerment include:

- making sure that team members understand how the outputs of the team contribute to the wider organization
- making sure that there are open and honest channels of communication between you and your team so ideas can flow freely
- acknowledging and rewarding contributions from team members
- sharing information that you have
- problem solving with your team.

ACTIVITY 7

What are/would be the advantages of your team members feeling empowered?

FEEDBACK

There are many advantages to empowerment. It tends to make teams more flexible and responsive to changes demanded by the external environment. Empowered teams are certainly more responsive to the customer, as customer complaints can be handled faster, without front-line staff needing to refer decisions to managers. Employees' self-esteem, motivation and morale increase. Effective and satisfying teamwork result in higher-quality output, as group pressure and cohesiveness promote higher standards than traditional supervision could. Employees' ideas are tapped and fed back into the organization; for example, employees close to the customers can identify gaps in product lines.

Training

Neither quality improvements nor empowerment will work without trained employees. The purpose of training in a quality initiative is not to teach people to do their jobs in a better way, but rather to give them the tools and skills so that they can discover better ways of doing their jobs themselves. After all, they are the experts. It involves:

- teams receiving training
- teams identifying problems in their own work area and suggesting solutions (sometimes in collaboration with experts, internal or external customers, or internal or external suppliers)
- teams trying out solutions
- workable solutions being established as standard practice
- teams continually refining and extending the improvements in their work area.

Training can sometimes appear expensive to organizations that have not invested in it before. Successful organizations, however, find that it yields a significant return on investment. Motorola, for example, a progressive organization, spends $100 million on training annually, and calculates that every $1 invested in training brings a return of $33.

Not every organization has the size or purchasing power of a Motorola, however. Organizations of every size need to ensure that they receive good value for their training expenditure. This can be bewildering given the range of training options on offer. A few guidelines should make the job easier.

Quality improvement groups

The training and empowerment of teams leads naturally to every member of the team actively striving to make improvements. This mindset can be formalized by teams meeting regularly once a week for an hour or so in order to discuss quality-related issues.

ACTIVITY 8

What support would members of your team need to meet to specifically consider improvements?

FEEDBACK

When quality improvement groups are being set up, support and training is often needed in:

- running meetings
- resolving conflict
- presenting findings.

In order not to get discouraged, team members should start by concentrating on a limited number of manageable issues. As they become more experienced in using their new skills, they will start to focus on identifying and generating solutions for work-related problems. If improvement groups become a regular feature of every team's working week, there will be a steady flow of improvements to team practices. Toyota, for example, estimates that its employees contribute 1 million ideas a year to the company.

Naturally, not every idea generated will be a world-class winner. Experts estimate that, on average, only one out of every sixty ideas is a good one. This means that the quality improvement groups must be encouraged to generate as many ideas as possible, and taught to screen them to capture the good ones.

Quality improvement groups form the grass-roots level foundation of any quality initiative. However, because their members are all from the same workteam, they can sometimes lack the wider perspective that contributes to process-wide improvements. For this reason, two other types of quality groups may be necessary in many quality initiatives:

- key process groups
- innovation groups.

KEY PROCESS GROUPS

In the initial stages of a quality initiative (such as the pilot phase), key process groups can be formed to analyse and suggest improvements to one or more of the major processes in the organization. These temporary, cross-functional groups are made up of the managers of every department involved in the process, along with representative employees familiar with the various aspects of the process. Their brief is to measure and analyse each stage of the process, and identify areas where improvements can be made. Once the group has made its recommendations, it is disbanded. A manager is then appointed to oversee the implementation of the improvements.

INNOVATION GROUPS

Innovation groups are voluntary groups of employees from various departments and levels in the organization. Their purpose is to find innovative and better ways of doing things. Such groups usually need to be led by facilitators specially trained in creativity and innovation techniques. As these groups are voluntary, they might meet outside regular working hours. Some organizations offer an incentive scheme, where successful innovations are rewarded by special bonuses.

ACTIVITY 9

How relevant would key process and innovation groups be in your organization?

FEEDBACK

Each organization will operate in different ways. However, the benefits of encouraging *everyone* across the organization to feel a sense of ownership and contribute to the evolution of the organization are common to all. We look at the practicalities of involving your team in making improvements to processes later in the workbook.

The following activity will help you to consolidate your learning from this section.

ACTIVITY 10

1 Why are people management skills important to a quality programme?

2 What is empowerment?

3 Outline the advantages of empowerment.

4 What is the major purpose of training in a quality initiative?

5 Outline the relationship between training in process skills and training in interpersonal skills in a quality initiative.

FEEDBACK

If you had difficulties with any question in the previous activity, refresh your memory by re-reading the relevant section. Or you might find it useful to discuss the issue with a colleague.

Learning summary

- 'Soft' people management skills are vital to the success of a quality programme. Effective people management motivates and enables employees to accept responsibility for the quality of their own work, to identify and solve problems, and to suggest improvements. The three major aspects of good people management in a quality initiative are empowerment of the workforce, training, and the use of quality improvement groups.
- Empowerment is a management method which gives as much responsibility and discretion to employees as possible. Routine job-related decisions are left in the hands of workteams, who also control the planning and scheduling of their own work. They may also participate in other administrative or staffing decisions and activities related to their own work-team. In empowered organizations, management shares information with employees, and ensures that they receive the training to interpret and use it in their work. The benefits of empowerment include greater flexibility, quality improvements, and higher morale and productivity. True empowerment is impossible unless an organization:
  - ensures that employees will not be punished or ridiculed for mistakes
  - empowers middle managers and supervisors as well as front-line workers
  - trains employees effectively.
- The procedure through which empowerment and training are applied in the workplace is a quality improvement group. Work teams meet regularly to discuss the application of their new problem-solving skills to their work, and to identify improvements. Such group meetings become a regular part of the weekly work schedule.
- Empowered workteams can implement many small-scale improvements without seeking the 'permission' of managers. Departmental managers, however, should monitor the improvements in order to:
  - ensure that they are not causing problems for other parts of the organization
  - measure their effectiveness
  - make sure that they are shared and applied as widely as possible.

- To reap the benefits of quality improvement groups, an organization must ensure that there is sufficient sharing of information both vertically and horizontally. Vertical communication is necessary to make sure that management responds quickly to a quality groups' suggestions. Horizontal communication ensures that learning and successful innovations are applied as widely as possible through the organization.

Into the workplace

You need to:

- Review your techniques for involving your team in improving the quality of the team's outputs.

Reference

1 Deming, W. E. (2000) *Out of the Crisis*, Massachusetts Institute of Technology

Section 3 Understanding processes

Introduction

In order to make the offering to the customer a reality, the organization has to have the right processes in place to enable the people to deliver.

The New Shorter Oxford English Dictionary defines a process as:

... a continuous series of actions, events or changes ... especially a continuous and regular action or succession of actions occurring or performed in a definite manner; a systematic series of actions or operations directed to some end.

So a process involves a number of **activities** or **transformations**, which are organized into a **specific sequence** and co-ordinated to achieve a **specific end** (or output). A process can be represented diagrammatically as shown in Figure 3.1.

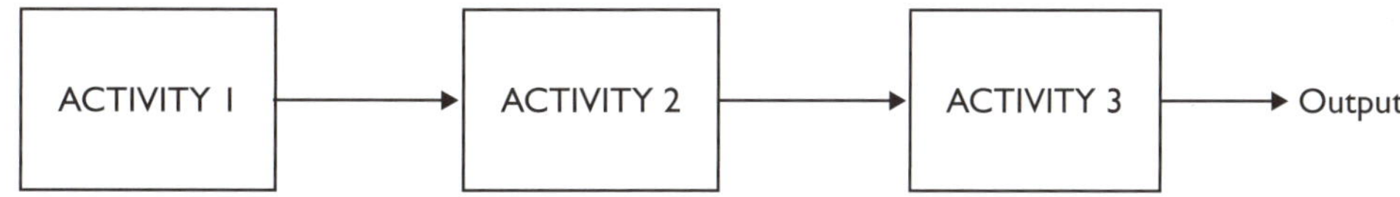

Figure 3.1 A simple process

For example, the process of booking your holiday might involve the following **activities**:

- discuss preferences
- research the possibilities
- draw up a shortlist
- make a decision
- book the holiday.

The **order** of the activities is significant – you wouldn't be able to book the holiday until you'd made a decision; and you wouldn't be able to draw up a shortlist until you'd researched the possibilities. To enable you to complete the activities, you'd require a number of **inputs** to the process, such as travel brochures (information), a pen and paper for the shortlist (tools and materials) and the money to pay for the holiday (funding). The **output** of the process is the holiday reservation. Figure 3.2 illustrates the process of booking a holiday.

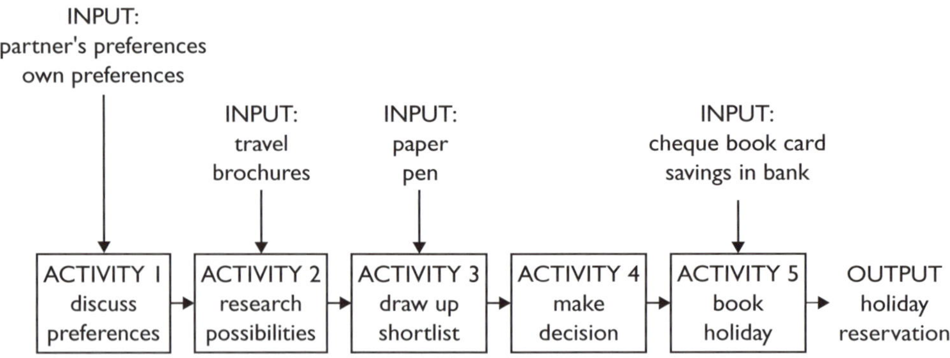

Figure 3.2 Booking your holiday

In this section we consider your team's processes and a systematic approach to identifying improvements.

Business processes

A business process is any process (including all the activities and all associated inputs) that an organization must carry out to deliver outputs to its customers. It doesn't matter whether yours is a profit-making or non-profit organization, public or private sector, large or small, you will achieve your objectives through processes of one sort or another. For example, in a hospital, processes might include diagnosing medical problems, carrying out essential surgery, and treating disease; the output would be a healthy patient. A publisher's processes might include commissioning, typesetting, and printing a book (the eventual output).

The writers and practitioners in business processes point out that there may be hundreds or even thousands of processes in an organization. However, even in the large multinational organizations there may be as few as twenty to thirty 'macro' processes. These are the major processes that operate the business and deliver outputs to customers, but each step of a macro process may be a smaller process in its own right. The smaller process can be broken down into activities, and these activities into tasks, and so on. So processes may be 'nested' like Russian dolls, one inside another.

ACTIVITY 11

Take a few moments to list the main outputs that your operation delivers. Name the processes associated with each output (e.g. booking a holiday, assembling a product, providing advice or information, collecting payment, solving customers' problems). Don't worry about the individual activities at this stage – we'll come to those later.

Output	**Processes**

FEEDBACK

You may have found it tempting to list your processes in terms of the functional areas or workgroups that perform them. Perceptions of activities are often strongly influenced by the traditional hierarchical structure of a functional organization – as seen on a thousand organization charts near you and illustrated in Figure 3.3. In this kind of set-up, information, authority and decisions flow vertically up and down each function. Interfaces between functions may be less well developed. The problem is that most processes flow horizontally.

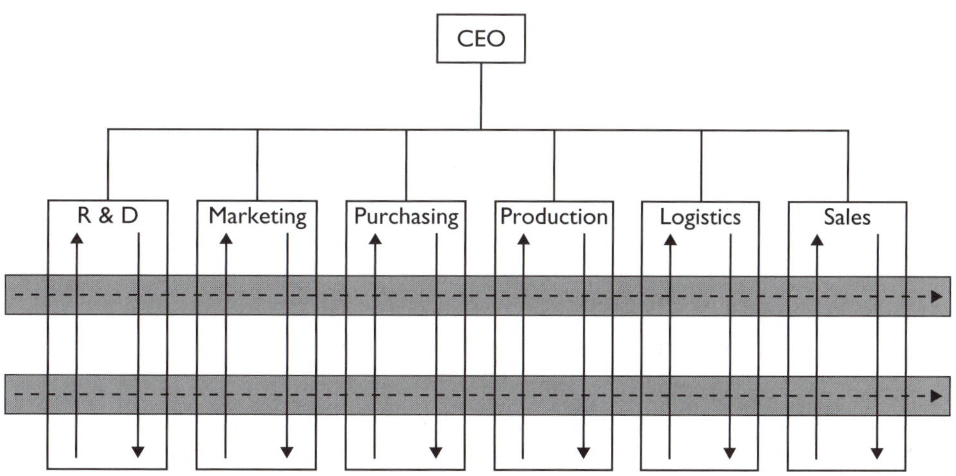

Figure 3.3 Functional hierarchy and the flow of processes

WHAT IS A PROCESS FOR?

Processes enable the organization to:

- achieve the organization's objectives, and
- deliver outputs for customers.

The processes that deliver actual goods and services directly to your **external customers** are the **core** processes. However, you may be unable to achieve these outputs without other processes within the organization – for example, resourcing, to ensure you have the staff to carry out the activities; purchasing, to buy the materials, tools and equipment inputs; or accounting, to manage the money required to stay in business. This second type of process is a **support** process. Support processes usually deliver their outputs to an **internal customer** – someone else inside the organization, who then uses these outputs in their own activity or process. In Figure 3.4, the output of the picking process (the items that were selected) becomes the input of the wrapping process.

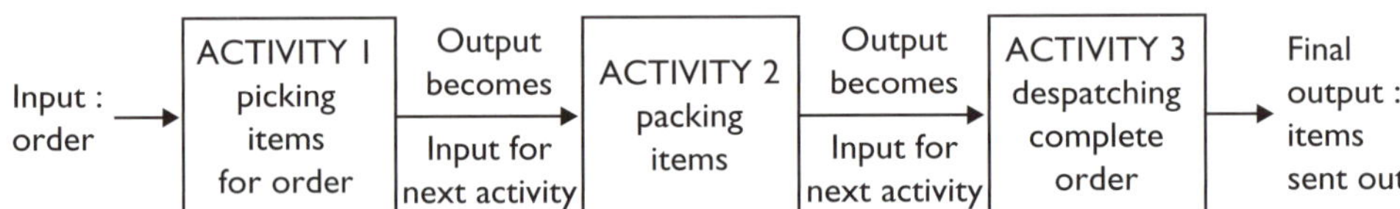

Figure 3.4 Process for order fulfilment from stock

A third type of process provides the framework through which people can achieve everything else. This is an **infrastructure** process; for example, setting and communicating the organization's mission, policies, values and strategies; leading and managing people; developing the business structure. These processes co-ordinate and direct activities, to minimize duplication and help everyone to pull in the same direction. Figure 3.5 illustrates how the three types of process fit together.

How you categorize your processes may vary from organization to organization. For example, if you are in retailing, you may consider the purchasing process core to your business. Selling may seem less central in a public service operation such as a library or a local council. It may also be difficult to decide quite where one process ends and another begins. Does the process of launching a new product start when you research the customer need, when you develop the product, or when you plan the customer launch?

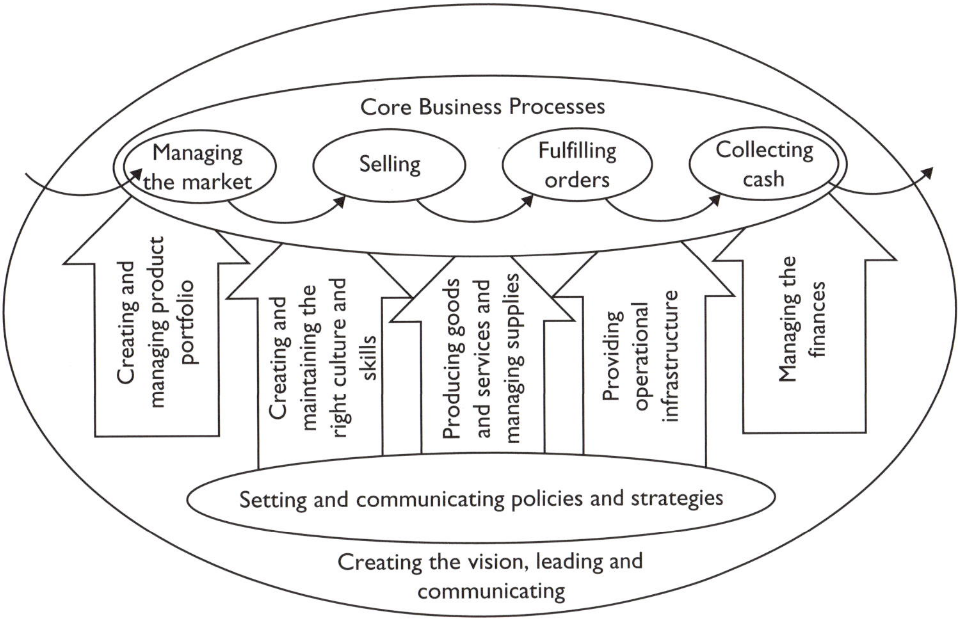

Figure 3.5 Three types of process

ACTIVITY 12

How do the processes you listed in Activity 11 relate to Figure 3.5? Which are core, which support, and which provide the infrastructure?

Type of process	**Process description**
Core	
Support	
Infrastructure	

How does Figure 3.5 help you understand the processes in your organization?

FEEDBACK

Obviously, we can't comment on how you categorized your processes; talk it over with a colleague if you find this helpful. You may have found that Figure 3.5 emphasizes the interdependence of many of these processes, which may be less obvious when you're in the middle of operating them from day to day.

For example, the arcane processes of the IT section of a large insurance company might seem rather distant from the output delivered to customers. However, difficulties or improvements in the IT capability may have a significant impact on the core processes (assessing risk, selling insurance, arranging cover, dealing with payments or progressing claims). The skills required to assess risk without computers, for example, might be very different. You would probably appoint a different kind of person and their training would be quite different. At the same time, without computers, misjudgements could be more likely; and the organization might lose out on poor risks. This in turn might increase the costs of insurances to customers.

Why manage processes?

If processes exist to enable the organization to achieve its objectives, and deliver outputs that customers want, then the better you do both these things, the greater your competitive advantage. The greater your competitive advantage, the more successful the organization is likely to be. But there are a number of factors working against you here, and this is why processes require management. The goalposts are constantly moving. Hannagan (1995) highlights four factors exerting pressure on organizations today:

1. **Turbulence** We live in turbulent times. The rate and scale of change in the marketplace, the economy, politics, society, legislation and the environment is relentless. What customers want and need is constantly changing. Even if your process was once world class, standing still while others around you adapt or anticipate means that you are losing competitive advantage.
2. **Technology** Automation, miniaturization, computerization, electronic communication: advances in technology have radically reshaped the way we work.

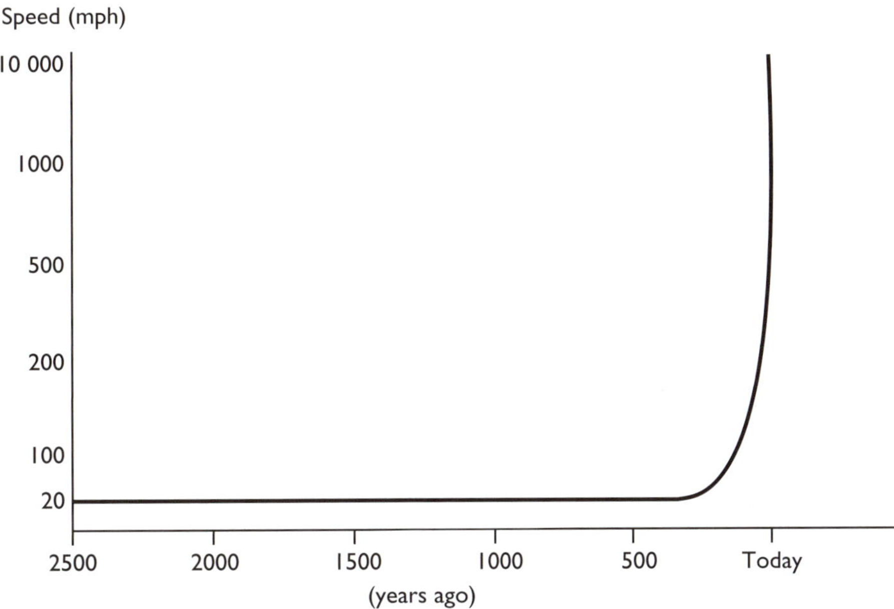

Figure 3.6 Rate of change in transport

Some jobs are redundant; others are created. Things are moving so fast that some equipment is obsolete before it reaches the organization. The organization with the latest equipment may have an instant advantage. For example, Figure 3.6 illustrates the rate of change in transport. For thousands of years, since humans first stood on their hind legs, the top speed at which humans could travel remained relatively unchanged – the speed they could run, or the speed of a horse, or carriage. Then, little more than 150 years ago, as steam power and then the combustion engine were invented, things hotted up; in the last 50 years, speed has increased exponentially. Today we have rockets that can reach Mars and even ordinary mortals travel on planes that are faster than the speed of sound.

3 **Time** Timespans for everything have shortened dramatically. It takes seconds to access information that used to require a lengthy search; electronic communication is practically instantaneous; product and service life cycles have shrunk to a fraction of what they were. Success depends not just on developing the right product or service, but on getting it to market quickly. It's not just a question of dealing with change, it's doing it NOW.

4 **Interdependence** We touched on this in the last activity, but as the environment changes, as technology improves, and as timescales shorten, interdependence increases – across processes, functional specialisms, and even organizations. Just-in-time techniques, for example, mean that you are depending on your suppliers to get you what you need when you need it. Some tasks or roles are no longer viable in-house and must be outsourced – think of cleaning or catering in the health service, for example. So changes in any one element may have consequential ripples through the organization and beyond.

ACTIVITY 13

Identify ways in which each of the following factors have influenced your organization in the recent past.

Turbulence

Technology

Time

Interdependence

PROCESS ENTROPY

There is another reason for active management of processes: process entropy. Over time, processes degrade and become less efficient.

Most processes evolve piecemeal. They may have been designed to deliver a specific output at a particular point in time, but as requirements and circumstances change, they are modified, expanded, dispersed across several workgroups. Responsibility may become muddied, so additional checks and balances are introduced at the cross-over points. 'Patches' are applied to fix recurrent problems.

Consequently, our business processes become ineffective, out of date, overly complicated, burdened with bureaucracy, labour intensive, time consuming and irritating to management and employees alike.

Harrington, p. 17[1]

For example, keeping employee records might have started life as a paper-based process. Computerization was introduced, and to start with (because people weren't sure how the system would work, and wanted to check it out), the paper records were maintained side-by-side with the new system. But somehow, no one was ever ready to relinquish the checks and balances, so the paper-based records never quite died out and now people operate both systems as a matter of course.

So after a while, it's worth critically reviewing your processes – even and especially the well-established ones – to make sure that there's not a simpler way, or a more effective way, or a quicker way, to achieve the same outcome.

After you've done a thing the same way for two years, look it over carefully; after five years, look at it with suspicion; and after ten years, throw it away and start all over again.

A. E. Pearlman, US railroad executive
cited in Harrison and D'Vaz[2]

ACTIVITY 14

How has process entropy affected any of the processes you identified in Activity 11?

So where do you start?

Process management begins with a fundamental reappraisal of the whys and wherefores of a process:

- Why are we doing this at all?
- Why do we do it in this particular way?
- Is there a better way to do it?

It sounds radical – and it can be. You may be challenging processes that have been enshrined in company lore for many years. The people who set them up may feel you are questioning their judgement. The people operating them may feel you are criticizing their performance. And the processes themselves go to the heart of what the whole organization is about.

These questions are just the start of managing processes. Because, of course, managing processes involves more than asking questions. It means finding the answers, and deciding what to do about them. It means managing whatever action is required to ensure that the process delivers its fullest potential. It means providing leadership and support for the people who must implement the process and any improvements. And it means setting up systems to keep you on track.

A FRAMEWORK FOR PROCESS MANAGEMENT

Below is a step-by-step framework that will help you manage and improve your processes. It's not original: it's simply one proven route map, to help you keep track of where you are now and where you're heading. There are seven steps in the framework:

1. **Identify critical processes** because you may have most to gain from improving these.
2. **Analyse processes** to work out exactly what's involved in each, and assess how well each process is currently working.
3. **Evaluate opportunities for improvement** as some improvements may bring greater rewards than others; the feasibility of others may be problematic. The skill lies in distinguishing the two, and prioritizing your efforts.
4. **Specify targets for improvement** because you need to know what you're aiming for.
5. **Plan and implement the improvement** as you would any project.
6. **Review the results** to check how the improvement has worked, and finally.
7. **Decide 'what next?'** because process management is not a one-off: it's a continuous and ongoing process itself which may best be illustrated by the process improvement cycle shown in Figure 3.7.

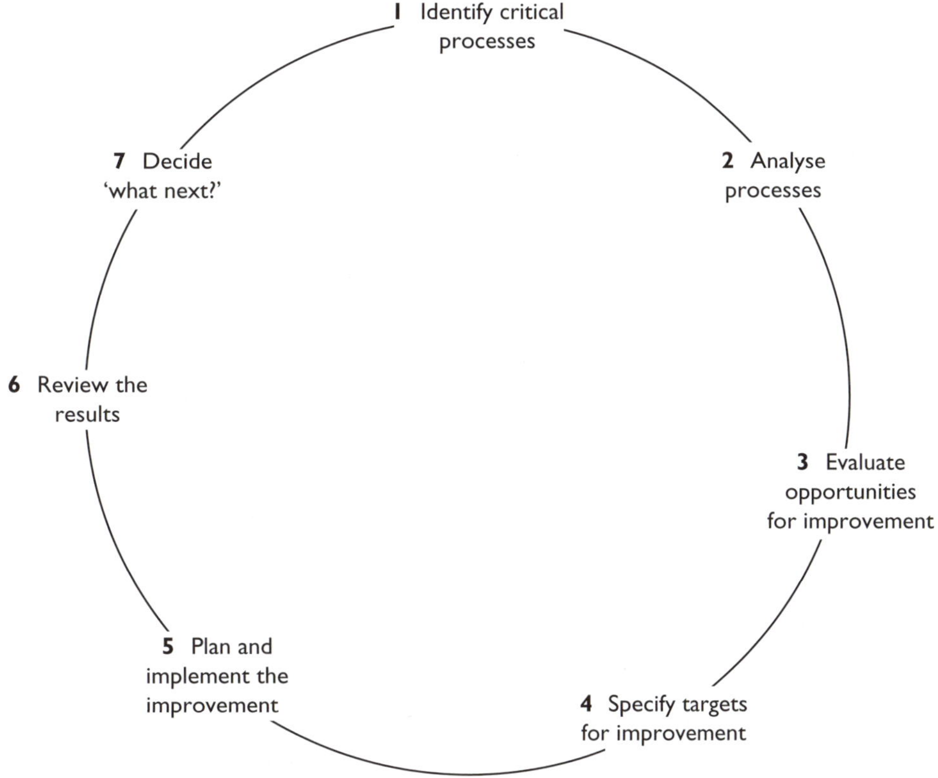

Figure 3.7 Process management framework

ACTIVITY 15

Take a moment now to think about where you are on the seven-stage framework, and the route ahead. What concerns does this approach to managing processes raise?

FEEDBACK

You may feel as though process management is a treadmill. You'll never be able to sit back and enjoy the fruits of your labour – the world is constantly changing, so processes will always need to be revised, updated, improved. In fact, process management is a continuous progression or spiral. You may come round to the same kinds of activities as you review and decide the next steps, but you have moved onwards and upwards. You have the satisfaction of seeing how far you have come.

Getting organized for process improvement

Most of the writers and experienced practitioners of process approaches – whether of the incremental improvement or radical re-engineering persuasion – have emphasized the importance of setting up a reporting and operating structure specifically for process activities.

If you want people to share an understanding and a commitment to the process, you have to create opportunities for them to meet, communicate, share problems, build solidarity, learn and work together. Processes may span different functional areas, different sites, and different viewpoints, even extending to your suppliers and your customers. The traditional functional hierarchy may make it difficult to communicate across the functional divides, never mind beyond the boundaries of the organization itself.

However, the average manager may have no mandate to reach across the fence and set up mixed process teams. Furthermore, the power protocol surrounding a matrix set-up, where vertical and horizontal team membership intersect, has always been problematic: who or what takes precedence? (See Figure 3.8.)

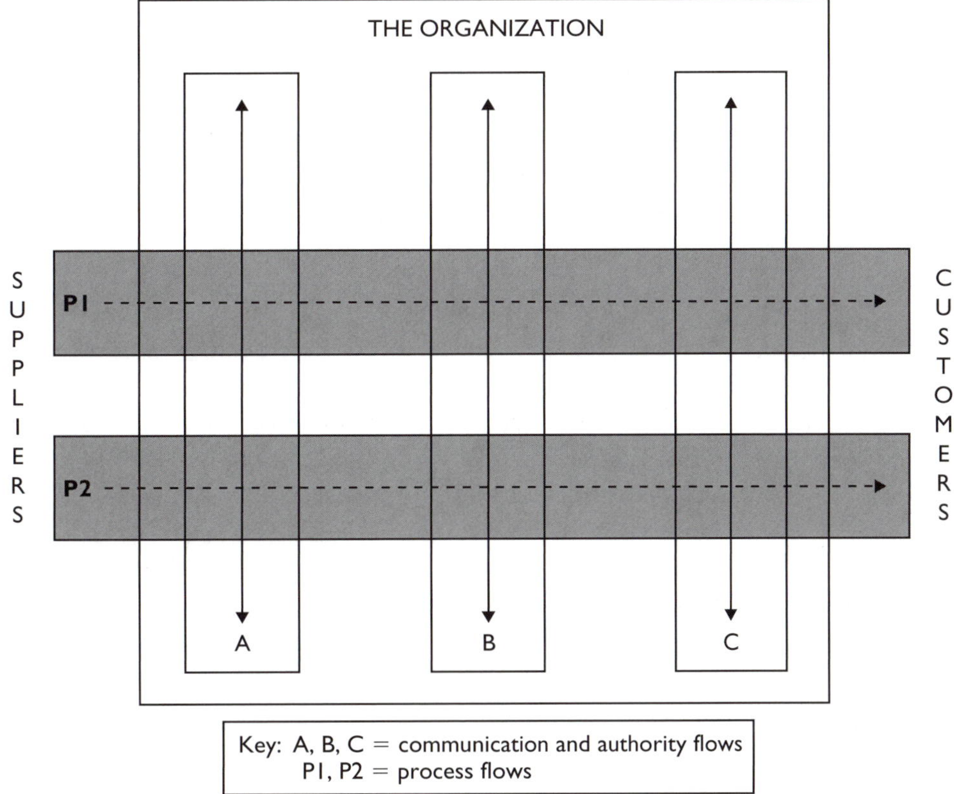

Figure 3.8 Who takes precedence?

A COUNSEL OF PERFECTION?

The business process experts have developed several variants of an alternative hierarchy of essential roles and responsibilities for successful process management, improvement or re-engineering. The formally instituted roles may not be immediately feasible in your organization. However, if you are operating on a process basis, even informally, you probably already have a network of people – the telephone numbers stuck on the wall by your phone, or the page in your process file, for example – who fulfil much the same kinds of role. These are your first port of call in the event of any difficulty or changes to the system.

Process champion (or sponsor)

A senior manager (preferably the chief executive) who:

- supports and authorizes the process efforts
- models the kinds of behaviour associated with process-led operations (focus on customer, collaboration, etc.)
- on a practical level, ensures that resources are made available for process efforts.

Steering committee (or executive improvement team)

A team of senior managers who:

- institute the process approach
- agree strategic priorities
- set up the individual process improvement teams
- maintain the overview on all process activity.

Process owner

The most senior manager with a vested interest in a specific process (and a portion of whose rewards are probably linked to its success). The process owner:

- agrees (with the process champion) the purpose and scope of improvement efforts on the process
- assumes responsibility for the process outcome
- agrees with the process improvement team the performance indicators (e.g. productivity) and measures (e.g. £ sales per head) on which the process will be evaluated
- co-ordinates and supports the process improvement team
- ensures that the team acquires the skills, knowledge and understanding of the process and the necessary tools and techniques
- progresses regular reviews and audits
- manages and co-ordinates connections with interdependent processes.

Process improvement team

The process improvement team comprises around eight people, drawn from the stakeholders throughout the process – including customers and suppliers – who specifically focus their attention on improving the process. They work to:

- document the process
- analyse current performance
- identify areas for improvement
- propose and evaluate improvements
- specify new targets and measures
- plan implementation of improvements
- review performance of improvements
- report progress to the process owner.

Process operators or process team

The process operators are all the people who actually operate the process and deliver the outputs to internal and external customers. Especially in a culture of empowerment, they may have significant opportunities to:

- document any subprocesses
- identify areas for improvement
- propose improvements
- implement improvements
- review performance
- report progress to the process owner
- fulfil their process activities.

ACTIVITY 16

For any major process you know, identify the personnel involved and their responsibilities. How well do their responsibilities match the role descriptions above?

Process

Person	Responsibility	Closest role description

Process mapping

To manage a process, you must first understand how it works. You may find when you start thinking about processes that no-one knows the whole story, or that it's difficult to get a picture of how it all fits together. Although processes are the way the organization meets customer wants and needs, and achieves its objectives (and are therefore of central importance to the organization) they span multiple dimensions:

- inputs (information, materials, ideas, etc. – including customer wants and needs)
- the activities or transformations (some of which may be processes or subprocesses in their own right)
- the people who do them (and the different functions to which they belong)
- the resources required to do them
- the time it takes to do them
- the order in which they are done
- where they are done
- the intermediate outputs at every stage (delivered to internal customers)
- the eventual output (delivered to the external customer).

People may only know the details of their own 'bit', but the effectiveness, efficiency and responsiveness of a process depend on co-ordinating all these bits and optimizing the process as a whole.

In many organizations, there are many individual groups all doing a good job. They are doing their own thing, very interested in meeting or beating their measurements, but not understanding or caring about how their activities affect others further down the line.

(Harrington, p. 15)[1]

It's no good improving individual activities without considering their impact on the rest of the process.

CASE STUDY

Imagine a biscuit factory increasing production without matching increases in packing capability. As the biscuits rolled off the production line, they would begin to stack up; the pressure on packers would increase. They'd probably be able to put in a special effort for a while, so they'd be sending more packs down the line. But sooner or later, the sheer volume produced might mean that unpacked biscuits would start to spill out over the hoppers and onto the floor. Product would be wasted. Packers would begin to get upset. They might slow down or even stop work altogether.

ACTIVITY 17

Thinking back to one of the critical processes you identified in Activity 11, what gaps can you identify in your knowledge of any of the factors in the checklist above? Who has the information you need?

Who knows, who cares, who can?

Each person involved in the process – from the supplier through every member of staff to the eventual customer – has a stake in it. Each probably knows their own element better than anyone else. If someone's been preparing and archiving microfiche records for the last 6 years, they have inside knowledge about that part of the records process which may be invaluable when you want to improve it. So it makes sense to harness their experience and seek their ideas for improving the system.

CASE STUDY

James Champy[3] tells the story of how some managers at Xerox learned this particular lesson the hard – and public – way. One of their copiers, the 3300, was proving unreliable. At the annual shareholders' meeting, an assembly line worker got up and said: 'We all knew the 3300 was a piece of junk. We could have told you. Why didn't you ask us?'. Production was immediately suspended and a team of stakeholders including assembly line workers began work to resolve the problems.

VESTED INTERESTS

Work may be a defining factor in how individuals see themselves, and in their sense of self-worth. Any changes may trigger powerful and often unconscious emotional reactions – such as suspicion, fear, resentment – which may block or seriously undermine any improvement efforts. The more you are able to involve people in improvement efforts that affect their work, the more likely they are to feel a sense of ownership, and approach any changes in a more positive way: with high hopes, energy and enthusiasm.

ACTIVITY 18

1 How do you think the people you identified in Activity 17 might feel about any changes to the process you have selected for improvement?

2 What are their priorities likely to be?

3 What do you think they each stand to gain?

BUILDING OWNERSHIP

One way you can build commitment to any changes is to get stakeholders involved in process improvement efforts from the start. This gives them a chance to work things out and recognize for themselves the need to change, so that resistance is minimized. It enables you to tap into their ideas early enough to be able to use them, and this not only builds ownership, it is likely to improve the quality of any changes you may make.

Operating a process that is ineffective, inefficient, or too rigid to meet customer needs can be a frustrating and undermining experience. People want to feel pride in what they do, to make a contribution. So involving people in improvement efforts can also increase personal job satisfaction, the quality of teamworking, and raise staff morale. By the same token, however, seeking their ideas and then ignoring them is likely to generate considerable bad feeling and disillusion.

AN OPPORTUNITY TO COLLABORATE

This workbook is about developing your own skills and understanding. But the framework for process improvement and the tools and techniques that go with it may be equally relevant for your team. Sharing them with your team may offer the opportunity for productive collaboration and consolidate your own learning.

You may wish to try out the tools and techniques for learning purposes on your own. Then, once you're comfortable with them, one of the best ways to begin understanding processes is to meet with the process stakeholders and pool your knowledge by documenting the process.

Putting it on paper

Given the complexities of processes, one of the easiest ways to get to grips with them is to draw them. Diagrams are compact; they simplify access; and they are precise. They are also pretty universal (once you are familiar with the conventions, what the different symbols mean, and so on). Take the electronic circuit diagram for a computer, or an architectural floorplan, for example. Each may be drawn on a single page. But just imagine how complicated it would be to communicate the same information in words – or to wade through those words to find the information you needed to solder a single connection or install the plumbing.

You can illustrate how a process works in flowcharts, also known as **process maps**. Process maps don't require any special drawing skills and only a minimum of special symbols. But they do help you to get an overview of the whole process, and how the different activities fit together.

CHECKING IT OUT

Once you've got the diagram in front of you, everyone will be working from the same information. You will be able to check out the order, the connections, the inputs and outputs at every stage, and who is responsible for them. The key questions for process management come into their own here:

- Why are we doing this at all?
- Why are we doing it in this particular way?
- Is there a better way to do it?

Process maps are also acceptable to BSI and other ISO 9000 accrediting organizations for describing the production, installation and servicing process that directly affects quality.

There are various different types of flowchart or process maps, depending on what kinds of details you want to show, and who the chart is for.

A SIMPLE START (FLOWCHARTS)

A simple flowchart illustrates the main activities and the order in which they must be done. Activities are represented by rectangles and the direction of the process flow by arrows.

First, decide which process you're going to work on, then identify all the activities involved. Start each activity with a verb or 'doing' word (such as 'choose', 'list', 'file' or 'repair'). Keep them as short and simple as possible. Arrange these activities into the order in which they occur. Then draw the diagram, as large as you can; write each activity in a separate box, with arrows between the boxes to show the direction of flow. Flowcharts are usually organized so that the flow moves left to right, or top to bottom.

To illustrate, the flowchart for the process of 'drawing a flowchart' might look something like Figure 3.9.

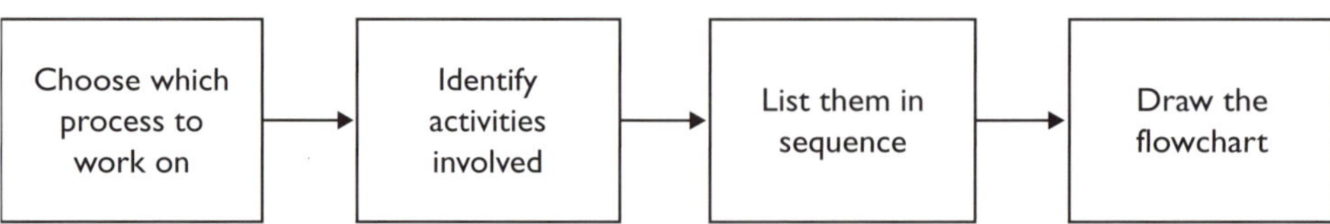

Figure 3.9 A simple flowchart

Pros and cons

On the plus side, this is a very simple and accessible way to present the information; even newcomers to the process should be able to grasp the essence of it. But it doesn't tell you who does the activities, or where, and it doesn't show the outputs or the inputs you need to achieve them.

ACTIVITY 19

Choose a simple process with which you are familiar and draw it using flowchart techniques.

ADDING THE FRILLS (INTEGRATED FLOWCHARTS)

Once you've got the basic shape, you can add in any information you need about inputs and outputs at various stages.

Don't draw this information in boxes like the activities – you'll need to distinguish them in some way. Write them in open brackets (as shown in Figure 3.10) or use a letter code and give details in the key. If you are drawing your chart top to bottom, set your inputs to the left, and specify the intermediate outputs (those that become the inputs for the next activity) on the arrows of the main flow. The result might look something like that shown in Figure 3.10.

In Figure 3.10, we have ignored any outputs that are not required later in the process. However, these can be included on the right-hand side of the central flowchart, using an open bracket or code letter, as for the inputs.

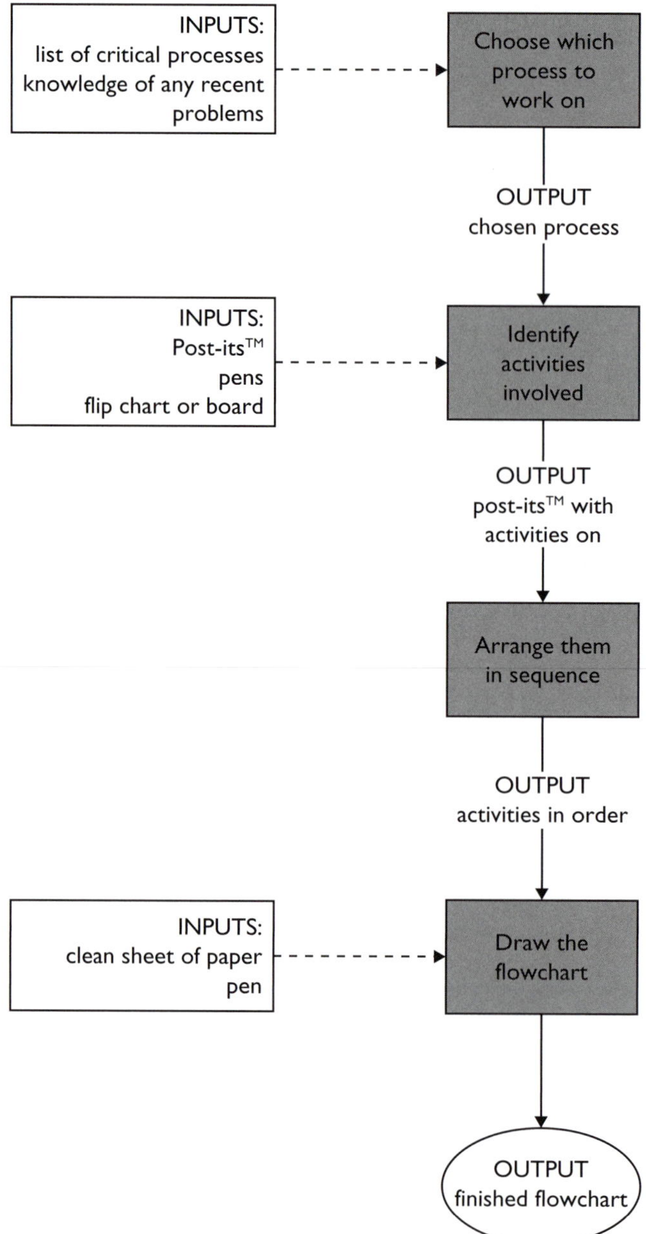

Figure 3.10 Integrated flowchart

Pros and cons

The flowchart is still quite clear, and you have included inputs and outputs, which are quantifiable, and which therefore may be compared against specifications or standards to monitor how you're doing and where any problems creep in. But you still haven't made it clear who does what, or where.

ACTIVITY 20

Take the flowchart you prepared for Activity 19, and add in the inputs and outputs where appropriate.

BUTTONS AND BOWS (LAYOUT FLOWCHARTS)

If **where** things happen is important – for example, if you're reviewing a particularly complex documentation process, where you need to track its path through the organization – then a **layout** flowchart may be what you need.

Here, the flowchart is superimposed onto a plan of the location. (You could equally well use a map, or a symbolic representation of diverse sites. Scale doesn't really matter, although it would be useful to have some indication of the relative distance of each activity from the next.) The activities are drawn in where they happen, and arrows join each to the next – wherever that might be. For example, a layout flowchart for sending out an invoice might look something like that shown in Figure 3.11.

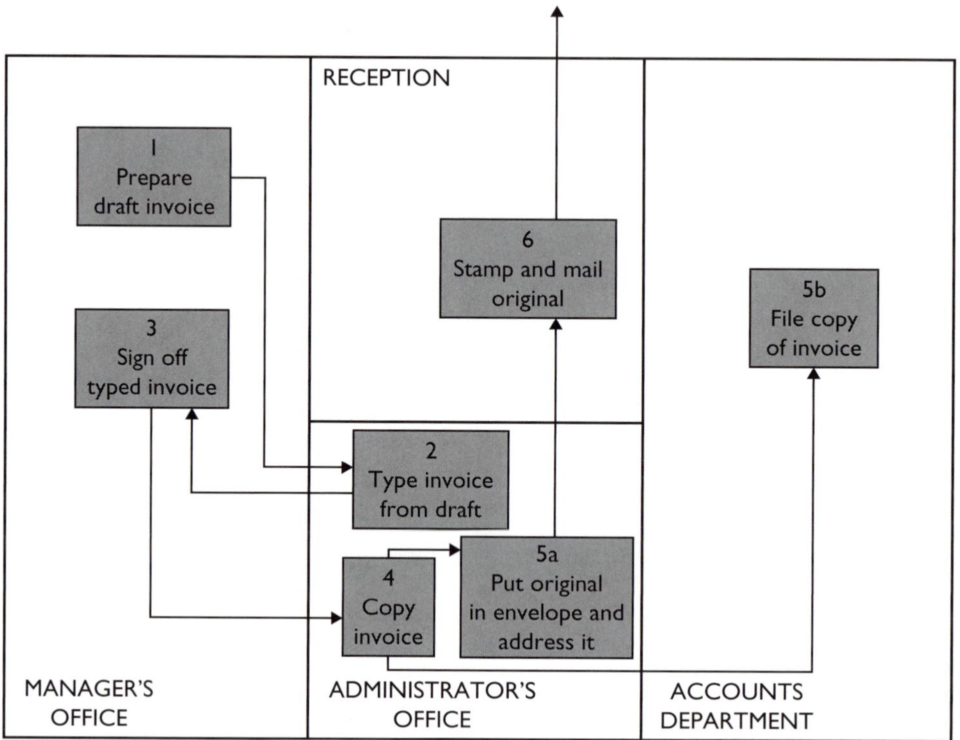

Figure 3.11 Layout flowchart

Figure 3.11 shows the floorplan of one part of the organization, with the manager's office on the left, the secretary next to him/her, and the accounts department on the far right. The manager prepares a draft invoice, which the administrator types up. Once it is approved, the administrator copies it, envelopes the original, and sends the copy to accounts, who then file it. Reception sends out the enveloped original. Each of the activities is numbered for ease of reference, and the direction of flow is indicated by the arrows. Notice that there are two outputs from Activity 4 – the copy and the original, which each then follow separate paths.

Pros and cons

This technique helps to highlight where work is being returned, or where transfers between departments or individuals may cause delay, or where the layout itself causes delay because the outputs have to travel further than they need.

ACTIVITY 21

Take a few moments to try the layout technique with a simple process with which you are familiar. Pick something that involves transferring the intermediate outputs from one location to another.

BELLS ... (DEPLOYMENT FLOWCHARTS)

If you need to get to grips with roles and responsibilities – who does what (and possibly when) – then a **deployment** flowchart is what you need. The page is divided into columns, representing each individual or group involved in the process. The activities are drawn in, sequentially as for a simple flowchart; but this time, each activity appears underneath the name of the person who does it. You'll end up with something like Figure 3.12.

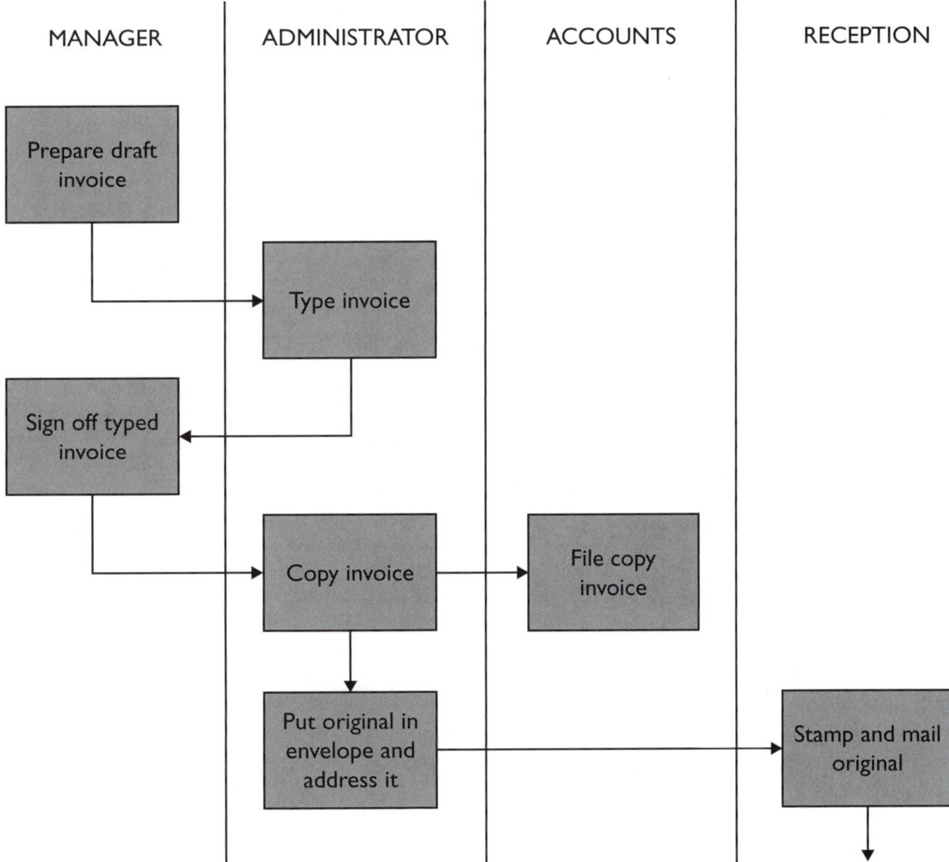

Figure 3.12 Deployment flowchart

Pros and cons

This kind of chart is relatively compact, and the columns make it easier to read than the layout flowchart. But it puts the spotlight on the handovers between individuals. Especially when used with some of the symbols (see Figure 3.13) it can reveal where problems or delays creep in. You can add timings down the left-hand side, to begin to quantify any delays, if that would be useful. Outputs can be included, and there are therefore obvious stages within the process where you can compare these against specifications, to check that the process is on target.

ACTIVITY 22

1 Redraw the simple process from your layout chart, as a deployment chart.

2 How does this change the information you can gain about the process?

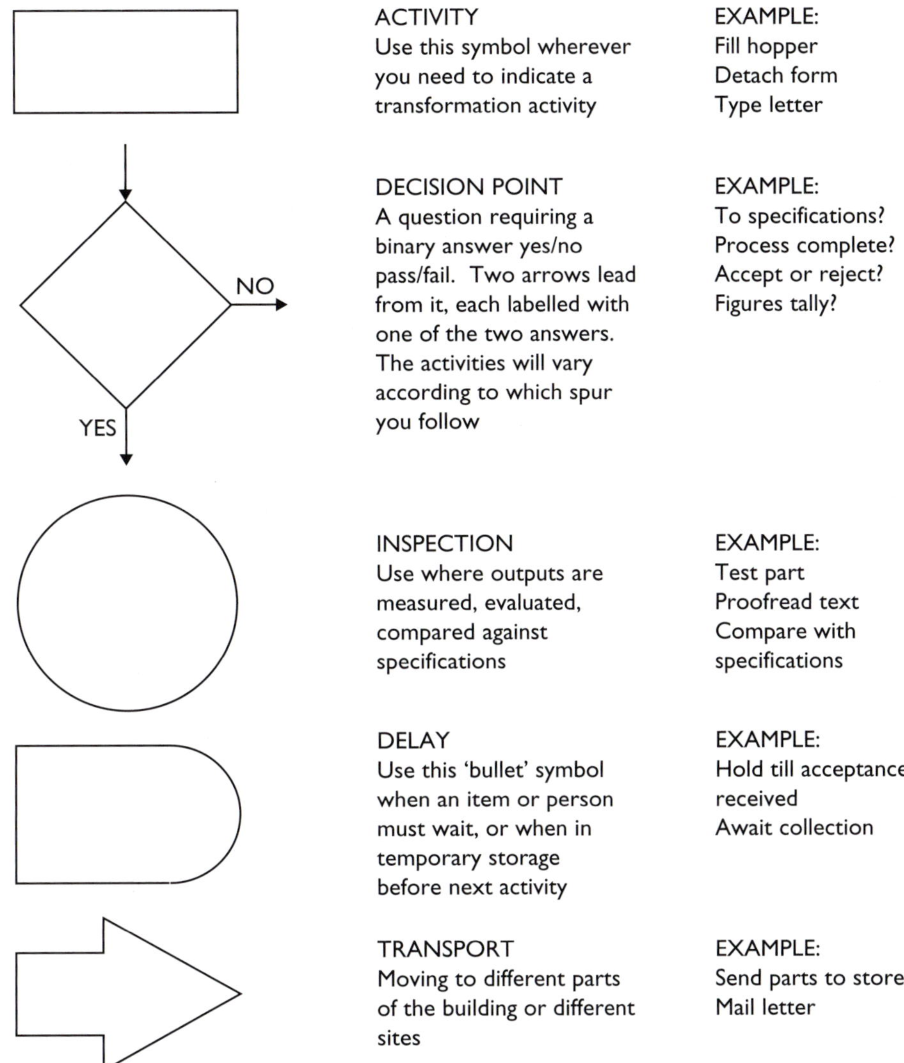

Figure 3.13 Some symbols for process maps (abridged and adapted from Harrington, pp. 96–98)[1]

... AND WHISTLES (EXTRA SYMBOLS)

It may help to use different symbols to differentiate various kinds of activity or transfer. There are a number of conventions: it makes little difference which you use, so long as you are consistent and the people who use the chart understand them. Figure 3.13 gives one version of some common symbols, and what they mean.

If the process is complex – or if there are subprocesses involved, which need to be documented in their own right – you may not be able to fit everything on the same diagram. When you get to the edge of the page (or the relevant subprocess), use an output connector symbol, and continue on a separate diagram, starting with an input connector showing the same letter code.

ACTIVITY 23

Which of these three types of flowchart will be most appropriate to document critical processes relevant to you? Bear in mind the audience for the flowchart – who will contribute to it, who will use it, and how they will use it.

A SNAPSHOT OF YOUR PROCESS

Once you are comfortable with the flowchart options and what the symbols mean, you are ready to start drawing your chosen critical process as it is right now. This is a kind of snapshot of how it is actually operating (rather than how you or others would like it to work, or how it is supposed to work).

The process map is best created by a group or team, with representatives of all stakeholders and all stages of the process (up to a maximum of about eight: beyond that, the meeting can get cumbersome – not to mention noisy!). Choose your members carefully and aim for a balanced team. Include sceptics, as well as those who are keen to try new techniques – they'll keep each other on their toes. Too heavy on the enthusiasts, and the risk is that vital implementation issues may be ignored. Too heavy on the sceptics, and you may find that you get bogged down, or that goals and objectives are not challenging enough.

Getting down to it

For these sessions, it's best to book a meeting room and get away from the usual work environment (perhaps even off site), so that you're not interrupted by phone calls or visitors. Give yourselves plenty of time – you'll have to judge this for yourself, but 2 hours might be the minimum for a relatively simple process that has not been documented before. You'll need Post-its™, pens, and a board or flipchart pad.

Start off by agreeing where the process ends – the final output to your internal or external customer – and where it begins. Then decide what kind of flowchart you're going to prepare, depending on the purpose of your chart, and the audience. Identify the activities involved, and write each on a separate Post-it™. (Remember that this exercise is about documenting the process as it currently operates – not what is supposed to happen: we'll come to that later.)

Stick the activity Post-its™, in the order in which they happen, on the board or flipchart (or wall – processes have a habit of spreading). When you all agree that the order and layout accurately represents your process, transfer it onto paper. Draw your finished diagram as large as reasonably possible, for ease of reference. As we suggested above, if your process is particularly large or complex, you may find it helpful to designate subprocesses with output connector symbols, then draw them separately. Figure 3.14 illustrates the process of creating a flowchart.

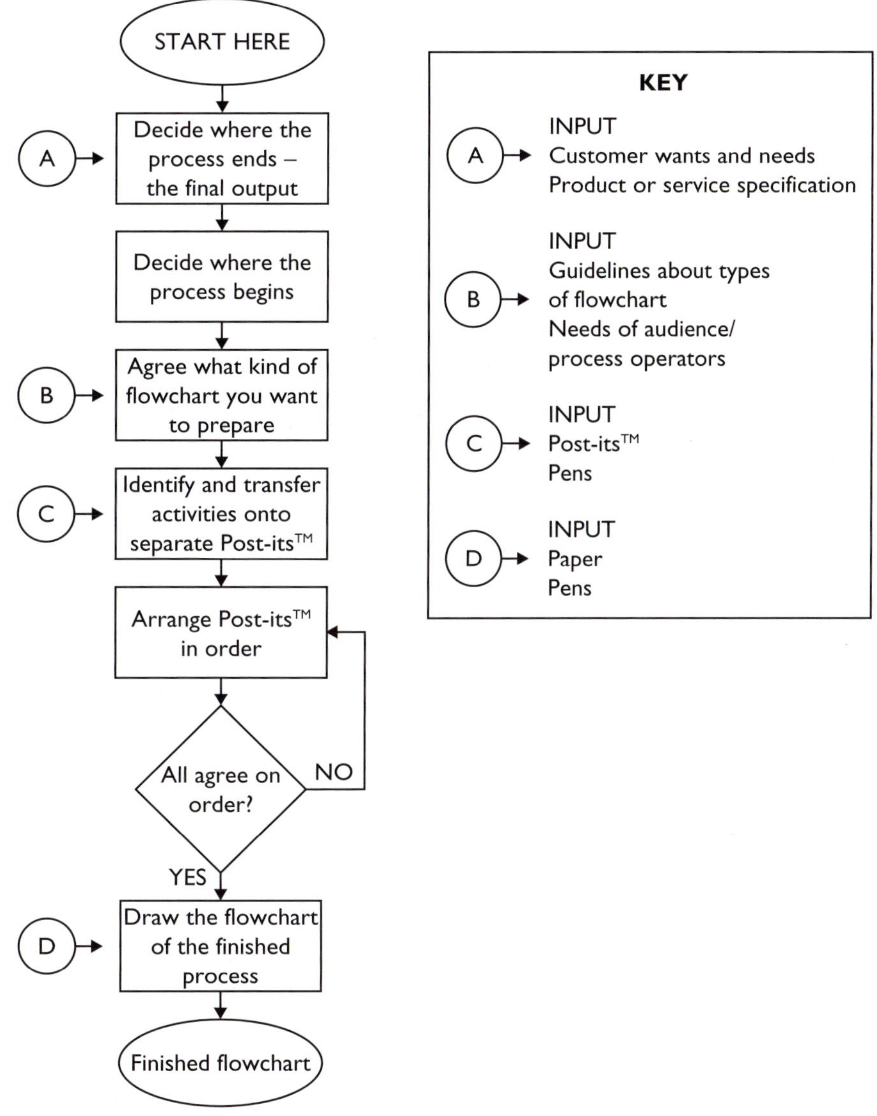

Figure 3.14 Creating your flowchart

Releasing the energy

This exercise is a real energizer: you may be amazed how lightbulbs suddenly go on in people's heads, as they see the whole picture, realize the whys and wherefores, and how their activities contribute to the output. Discussions may grow quite heated as you arrange the Post-its™ and the flowchart emerges. People are talking about something in which they have a stake, so they may feel vulnerable, angry, defensive, even passionate. Try to focus on the actual activities, rather than the individuals concerned; it's not a question of blame or fault.

ACTIVITY 24

You've had the theory; now it's a question of doing it.
EITHER

if you feel ready to tackle it, get together with your team to diagram your critical process
OR

try to draw your critical process on your own, and then make some time to go through it with someone who is involved in the process. How far does your diagram reflect their understanding of the process? Ask them to question you on any point that isn't clear, and adjust your process map accordingly, so that it is clear enough for even a novice to read and use.

Learning summary

- A business process involves a series of activities that transform inputs into outputs. Core processes deliver outputs directly to the external customer and support processes enable them to do so, while infrastructure processes create the organization itself.
- Quality is a reflection of the fit between what customers want and what you deliver (your output). The better the fit, the more likely it is that your organization will attract and retain customers. But external and internal pressures for change mean that the goalposts are moving. Managing processes is therefore an ongoing activity, constantly monitoring and improving to ensure that processes stay effective, efficient and responsive.

- The key questions are: why are we doing this at all? Why do we do it in this particular way? And is there a better way to do it? Then it's a question of finding the answers, deciding what to do about them, planning and implementing action, and reviewing progress.
- Process practitioners recommend an alternative hierarchy to facilitate process efforts and overcome the barriers to effective teamworking that may stem from traditional organizational structures. The process champion authorizes, endorses and resources the efforts. The steering committee plans and co-ordinates process efforts across the organization. The process owner is responsible for a specific process; the process improvement team works on improving it; and the process operators implement the process and deliver the outputs.
- If you want to manage something, you must first understand it. It's vital to develop a holistic understanding of your business process, and the context in which it operates, before you can begin to manage or improve its outputs. People often know only their own 'bits', so it is a question of combining the knowledge and perspectives of all stakeholders.
- **Process maps** or **flowcharts** are one of the most effective tools to develop and share understanding of the process as a whole, its inputs and outputs, who does what, where and when. They may help to reveal inefficiencies and waste, duplication and gaps.
- The simple flowchart diagrams the main activities and the order in which they are done. Inputs and outputs may be added, and special flowchart symbols used to signify different types of activity or other elements of the process. **Layout flowcharts** use maps or floorplans to illustrate where activities occur, and the journey that internal or intermediate outputs must take to create the eventual output for customers. **Deployment flowcharts** reveal individual responsibility and handover points.
- Once you have selected your critical process, the next step is to diagram your process **as it is now** rather than how you would like it to be, or how it is supposed to be. Doing this with your team can help to build team energy and enthusiasm, and develop ownership and commitment to any changes.

Into the workplace

You need to:

- identify your team processes and what they contribute to the organization
- document existing processes using process mapping techniques
- identify the relevant people to assist in the process mapping process.

References

1 Harrington, H. J. (1991) *Business Process Improvement*, McGraw-Hill

2 Harrison, P. and D'Vaz, G. (1995) *Business Process Re-engineering, Management Direction Series*, Institute of Management

3 Champy, J. (1995) *Re-engineering Management*, Harper Collins, p. 93

Section 4 Identifying process improvements

Having documented the process as it now operates, the next step is to identify where any problems, inadequacies or potential for improvement occur in the process – whether inherent in the process itself (including its outputs), in the people who operate it, or in the systems that support it. Then you can generate ideas for correcting them.

Streamlining

Putting together the process diagram often releases quite an impetus for action: people want to get on and do something *NOW*. Indeed, the diagram may have revealed some immediate opportunities for improving the process. These are likely to be ways of doing the same thing, better: more efficiently, using fewer resources, or more quickly. Harrington[1] refers to these types of solutions as **streamlining**.

QUICK WINS

You may have spotted opportunities to:

- **eliminate duplication** (e.g. both personnel and the manager keeping separate paper-based records on employees)
- **eliminate redundant steps** (and especially bureaucratic paperwork) which add no value for the organization or the customer (e.g. keeping paper-based records as well as computer-based records)
- **smooth the process** by reducing handovers or transportation to different sites
- **improve the layout** through which the outputs must flow, so as to reduce the distance between sequential activities
- **simplify the process** by reducing the number of steps
- **process in parallel** (where different people or areas complete different activities at the same time, rather than sequentially)
- **automate or computerize** any part of the process.

You may be surprised just what comes up:

Some of the changes seemed obvious in hindsight, but they're the kinds of things you overlook in the day-to-day stresses of running a business. When you step back and pull the whole process apart, suddenly they leap out at you.

(Ron Rittenmeyer, Frito-Lay Business Systems, quoted in Champy, p. 136)[2]

These quick wins should be valued; some of them may produce very substantial benefits for the organization. Before pursuing any of your ideas, you'll need a chance to see how they fit in with other improvements that may be required. However, people may feel they're still 'on the agenda' until you deal with them, so it's worth making a point of encouraging discussion to generate creative and imaginative ideas for quick wins and listing them for later consideration.

ACTIVITY 25

What opportunities can you immediately see in your process map (Activity 24) for quick wins? Make a note of these.

ERROR-PROOFING

If you wanted to do everything wrong in your process, what would you do? Error-proofing involves identifying possible sources of error or problems, and then making it difficult to make these mistakes.

For example, window envelopes may prevent snarl-ups on the printer, or letters being sent to the wrong people. Having the photocopier automatically return to standard single copies after a short delay means people are less likely to end up with multiple copies or magnification they don't want, simply because they didn't check before copying. If the task is complex, what about breaking it down into smaller chunks, or providing some kind of job aid to help get it right?

ACTIVITY 26

What opportunities can you see for error-proofing your process? Make a note of your ideas.

CRITICAL EXAMINATION

The critical examination matrix (Figure 4.1) offers a more structured approach to challenge every activity on the process map – including delays, transportation and storage. This can be quite time consuming, but because it is so thorough and systematic, it will ensure that you don't miss any possibilities.

WHAT is done?	WHY is it done?	What ELSE could be done?	What else SHOULD be done?
HOW is it done?	WHY that way?	How ELSE could it be done?	How else SHOULD it be done?
WHEN is it done?	WHY then?	When ELSE could it be done?	When else SHOULD it be done?
WHERE is it done?	WHY there?	Where ELSE could it be done?	Where else SHOULD it be done?
WHO does it?	WHY them?	Who ELSE could do it?	Who else SHOULD do it?

Figure 4.1 Critical examination matrix

ACTIVITY 27

Use the first three columns of the critical examination matrix (Figure 4.1) to challenge every step of your process. What possibilities does this reveal for improvement?

More challenging possibilities

The quick wins and critical examination techniques outlined above are likely to generate ideas based on the existing process. But two other techniques may help to generate more innovative and challenging possibilities.

FISHBONE DIAGRAM

The vast majority of problems occur over and over again because the ***root cause*** *is not established or eradicated.*

(Fowler and Graves, p. 75)[3]

For more complex errors – or problems that have cropped up repeatedly – the **fishbone** or cause-and-effect diagram may help you get to the bottom of what's actually going on. It may be useful, for example, in working out the root causes of:

- **rework and returns** where a proportion of outputs are regularly returned to an earlier stage because they aren't up to standard
- **delays** where an output ends up waiting or not being worked on for any period
- **long cycle times** (from start to finish of the process).

The fishbone diagram is a technique that's probably best conducted with the team, to get several different perspectives on the problem. Use as large a board or piece of paper as you can. Draw a 'fish skeleton' right across the page, with a head, a backbone, and four or six main bones branching off it.

Write your problem or error in the fish head. Label the main bones with the main factors you see as contributing to the problem. Alternatively use the standard 'PEM/PEM' prompts, as shown in Figure 4.2: People–Environment–Methods; Plant–Equipment–Materials (or the 4M prompts: Men, Materials, Methods, Machinery). Your diagram should look something like Figure 4.2 before you start.

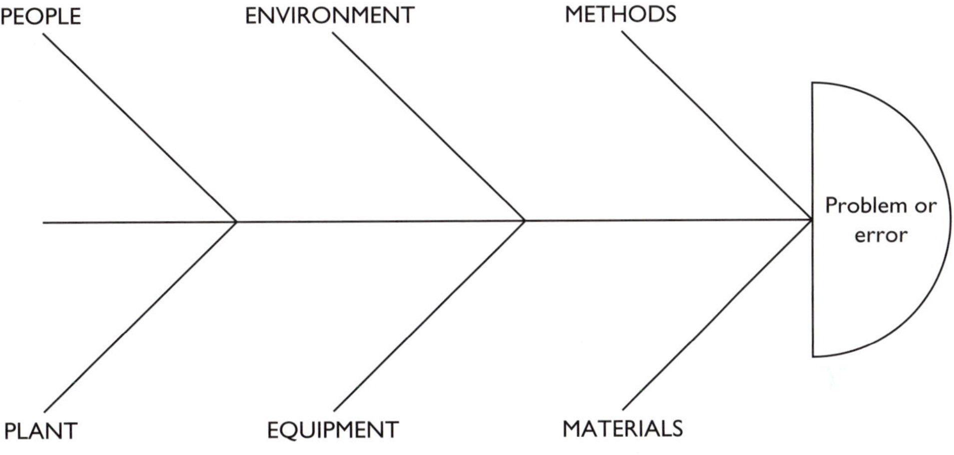

Figure 4.2 Fishbone diagram

Next, creatively think of ideas as to the causes of the problem and write each up on a smaller bone feeding into the appropriate main bone. (It may be easiest to write them onto Post-its™ first, so that you can move them around and alter the order.) Your diagram might end up looking something like Figure 4.3.

Pursue each cause to the limit – keep asking WHY? Why are people the problem? Because they are untrained. Why are people untrained? Because people are too busy to train them. Why are people too busy to train others? Because they are overloaded. Why are people overloaded? Because they're covering for absent staff (and so on).

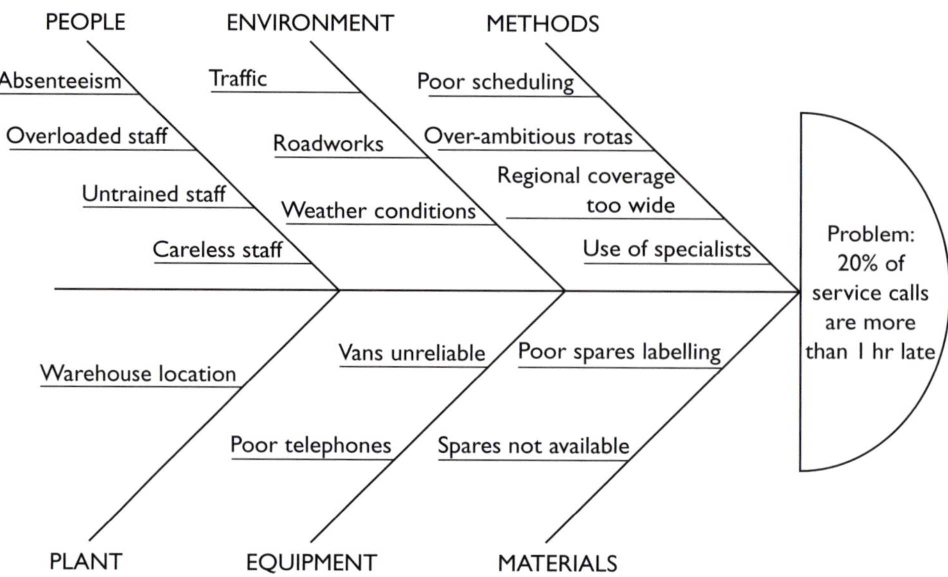

Figure 4.3 Updated fishbone diagram

ACTIVITY 28

Take one error or problem that has occurred repeatedly, and do a fishbone diagram to uncover the root causes. Once more, make a note of any ideas this triggers for improving the situation.

PROCESS CYCLE TIME

There may also be considerable gains from improving the cycle time – the total length of time it takes for the process to run from start to finish. The cycle time is usually considerably longer than the time for each of the individual activities added together. Take a look at this simplified example of a memo-writing process to see how:

Activity	Activity time (hours)	Cycle time (hours)
Manager writes memo	0.2	0.2
Secretary collects mail for typing (twice a day, average delay 12 hours)	0.1	12.0
Delay: secretary is busy, can't type immediately. Average waiting time 26 hours		26.0
Secretary types memo and sends for signature	0.3	0.3
Manager signs memo (twice a day) and returns for mailing 5 p.m.	0.1	12.0
Secretary collects memo 9 a.m.	0.1	16.0
Delay waiting for next trip to copier		5.0
Secretary copies memo, addresses envelopes	0.3	0.3
Secretary takes memo to mail at 5 p.m.	0.1	2.7
Total	1.2	74.5

(Adapted from Harrington, 1991, p. 126)

While the activities themselves only took a total of 1.2 hours (1 hour and 12 minutes), the total cycle time – the time it actually took to deliver the output – was more than 3 days.

Cycle time is what your customer sees, whether it's the time:

- from sending off the mail order form, to receiving the goods
- from arriving at casualty department with a broken wrist, to leaving with a plaster cast
- from paying in the deposit, to the date it is credited in the bank.

Reducing the length of time taken to complete each individual activity may not benefit the customer if it doesn't lead to reductions in the cycle time. Reducing the cycle time can make a dramatic difference for the customer. Harrington (p. 105)[1] cites the example of IBM who reduced cycle time by 30 per cent in one area – and gained themselves a 300 per cent increase in sales.

Different outputs?

However, all these improvement efforts may be in vain if the process doesn't deliver the outputs that customers want in the first place. If the output is wrong, customers will still be dissatisfied even if you deliver it more quickly or more pleasantly, or whatever. So the key question is: does the process deliver the outputs that customers actually want at every stage?

Your output to customers is much more than the product or service the organization is nominally providing:

Customers ... expect every interface to be a pleasure. They expect the salesperson to be friendly and knowledgeable, the salesroom clean and pleasant, the bills readable and accurate, the package attractive and easy to open, the service people responsive and competent, the phones answered on the second ring and not to be put on hold.

(Harrington, p. 5)[1]

CUSTOMER EXPECTATIONS

Customers buy into the whole package, which includes:

- the product or service itself (is this formally specified; what leeway or tolerance is there in this specification?)
- the cost
- the people who deliver it (how they look, the way they dress, speak, behave, and treat the customer)
- the phone, e-mail or other, computerized contacts (how long will it take to respond?)
- the paperwork
- the surroundings in which the product or service is delivered
- the follow-ups (including what you will do if anything does go wrong?)
- how long the transaction takes
- the cycle time from order or service request through to delivery
- how long the product or service lasts.

For example, expectations of the police force might include not chewing gum or smoking while dealing with members of the public; keeping to the speed limit (except when on emergency); answering phone calls by the fourth ring; despatching assistance to emergency calls within 10 minutes of call received.

Internal customers have similar kinds of expectations. Consider a report that your manager wants from you on some key aspect of your work. He or she is likely to have specified the purpose, the scope, the delivery date; but there may also be implicit expectations about the size and colour of paper you use, the font and format in which the text is drafted, the number of copies you supply.

These expectations should inform and shape the process:

A correctly-designed business process has the voice and perspective of the customer 'built in'.

(Davenport, p. 15)[4]

Champy suggests:

Define your standards and objectives from your customer's point of view. They'll be impossibly ambitious as a result, but in striving to meet them you may well achieve the 'impossible'.

(Champy, p. 137)[2]

ACTIVITY 29

1 What standards does your customer expect from your process? Take some time to run through the checklist of customer expectations and try to specify them in as much detail as you can.

2 How 'reasonable' are these expectations?

3 Have you actually agreed these together (or is it just a wish-list on their part, or a guess on yours)?

4 If not, how could you bring them to the table for negotiation?

5 How could you set these kinds of standards for your suppliers?

6 Bearing in mind the expectations you have just identified, how does what you currently deliver compare?

A clean slate

If the output customers want is very different from the output you currently deliver – or if it's a completely new output – you may need to wipe the slate clean and design the process from scratch, starting with the customer and working back through the organization. Re-engineering imagines that you have no technological, financial, human, or geographical constraints and just seeks the best way to deliver the output.

WHERE RE-ENGINEERING FITS IN

Macdonald[5] sets out the spectrum of business process efforts as ranging from:

- **incremental improvement** (tweaking and improving existing processes to do the same thing better – as promoted by Kaizen and total quality approaches), through
- **process re-design** (focusing on major processes and the output for customers, this challenges and rationalizes existing processes, to optimize the available resources and technology), to
- **process re-engineering** (creating a completely new network of core processes and priorities) which involves (Figure 4.4):

The fundamental rethinking and radical design of business processes to achieve dramatic improvements in critical contemporary measures of performance such as cost, quality, service and speed.

Hammer and Champy[6]

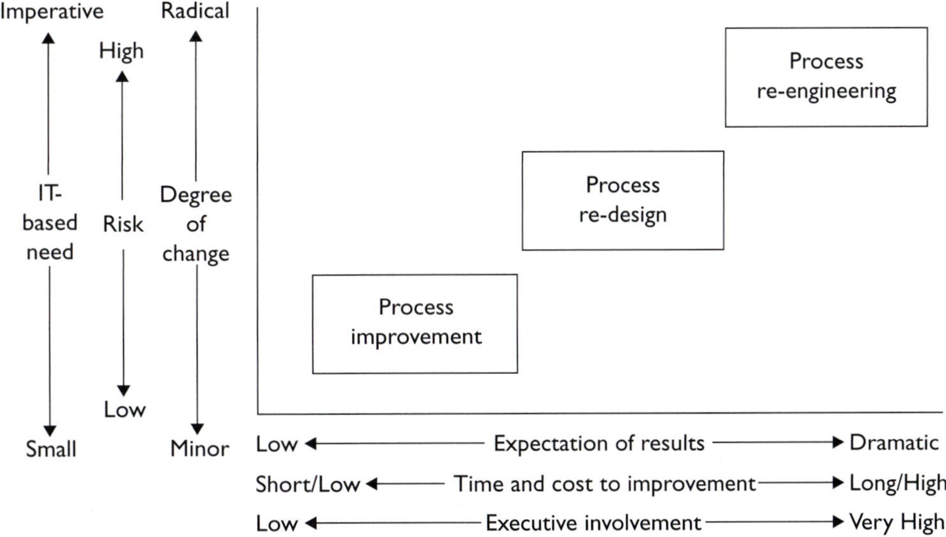

Figure 4.4

Essentially, the techniques and tools are the same as those for process improvement and the process looks similar on paper as shown in Figure 4.5.

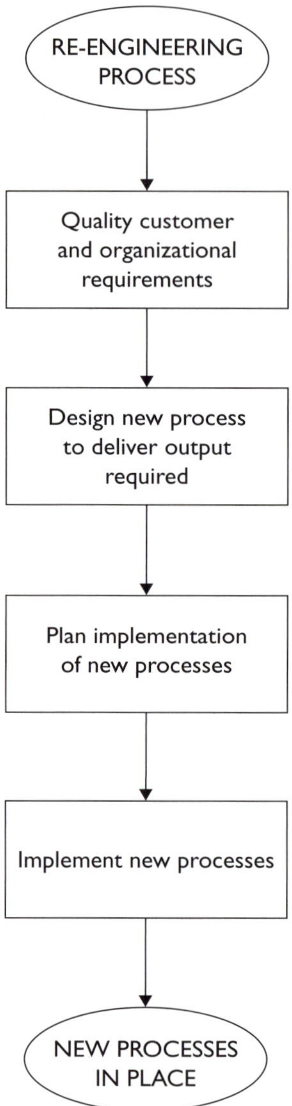

Figure 4.5 Re-engineering process

Process re-engineering is likely to radically change the way the organization is structured, what it delivers, and how it delivers it, as well as the way people are managed. It is generally considered the choice of organizations whose continued existence might be in doubt if they did not reinvent themselves. Champy[2] suggests that there are two main reasons for undertaking re-engineering: greed and fear (and the greatest of these is fear ...).

ACTIVITY 30

Where do you think your organization's process efforts would lie on the spectrum between incremental improvement and process re-engineering?

Why?

In practice, most organizations will combine process re-engineering with process improvement; quick wins will build momentum for the initiative; and once the processes have been re-engineered, continuous improvement will be essential to sustain results.

Learning summary

- Once you have documented and got to grips with the process **as it is now**, you can begin to work out where improvements are required, and what form these may take.
- The process map may highlight opportunities for **streamlining** – eliminating duplication and redundant steps, smoothing and simplifying the flow, or changing the order to parallel process different tasks. **Error-proofing** is another technique to reduce variance and standardize outputs in the process. **Critical examination** offers a comprehensive and systematic approach, challenging every element of the process.
- More innovative possibilities may be generated by focusing on ways **to shorten the cycle time**; or using the **fishbone diagram** to get to the bottom of problems and identify root causes (as opposed to presenting symptoms).
- Such incremental improvements may be insufficient, however, where the current process is delivering the wrong outputs for customers or the organization. Re-design or **radical re-engineering** may be required, starting with a definition of customer requirements, and then working back through the organization to create the process that will deliver them.

Into the workplace

You need to:

- identify quality checkpoints along your team's processes
- select appropriate measures
- benchmark processes against similar processes elsewhere in the organization or in external organizations.

References

1 Harrington, H. J. (1991) *Business Process Improvement*, McGraw-Hill
2 Champy, J. (1995) *Re-engineering Management*, Harper Collins
3 Fowler, E. and Graves, P. (1995) *Managing an Effective Operation*, Institute of Management, Butterworth-Heinemann
4 Davenport, T. H. (1993) *Process Innovation: re-engineering work through information technology*, Harvard Business School Press
5 Macdonald, J. (1995) *Understanding Process Re-engineering in a Week*, Institute of Management, Hodder and Stoughton
6 Hammer, M. and Champy, J. (2001) *Re-engineering the Corporation: a Manifests for Business Revolution*, HarperBusiness

Section 5 Measuring for improvement

Introduction

Having documented the process as it now operates, the next step is to identify potential for improvement in the process. In this section we explore the opportunities that the process mapping exercise has revealed to check outputs during the process and identify what to measure. Finally, we review the opportunities presented by benchmarking to compare your processes and outputs with similar processes in your own organization and beyond.

Why measure?

Measurements are key. If you cannot measure it, you cannot control it. If you cannot control it, you cannot manage it. If you cannot manage it, you cannot improve it.

(Harrington, p. 82)[1]

If processes exist to enable the organization to achieve its objectives and deliver outputs for customers, the better you do both these things, the greater your competitive advantage.

Knowing how you are doing – and where you are falling short – enables you to:

- understand the process better
- decide whether you need to change it
- decide how you need to change it
- evaluate the impact of changes
- sustain service and quality levels
- plan schedules for delivery.

… so that you can improve the process and the way the output is delivered – and thereby increase your competitive advantage.

The advantage of measures is their objectivity: it's harder to argue with quantified evidence of below-par performance, or the need for process change. On the other hand, not everything can be measured in this strictly quantified way. If you focus attention only on things that can easily be measured you may end up measuring the wrong things.

ACTIVITY 31

Identify some reasons why people might be reluctant to measure.

FEEDBACK

In many instances, measurement simply doesn't happen because:

- people don't realize **why** it's important
- they don't know **what** to measure or **when**
- they don't know **how**
- they haven't got the **time**
- they haven't got the **money** (and measurement alone adds no value to the output)
- they haven't got the **staff or other resources** (and unless someone takes responsibility, it won't happen)
- there's **nothing in it for them** if they do (and it may actually be penalizing them if they're not recognized and rewarded for doing the checks, and it stops them achieving their core tasks on which they are appraised).

ACTIVITY 32

What is the major obstacle to measurement of processes in your department?

What do you measure?

Specific indicators can be identified that accurately correlate with efficiency or effectiveness (or lack of them) in the process or its outputs. Appropriate **metrics** (units of measurement) can then be decided for the indicators and the **standards** required, or the **range** of acceptable results. Then it's a question of measuring the indicators to evaluate actual process performance.

Management is responsible for providing sound measurement systems and appropriate feedback to help all do their jobs better. Management signals what is important by measuring the results.

(Harrington, p. 169)[1]

Measurements might include the following indicators:

- size
- quantity
- accuracy
- customer satisfaction (expressed as a rating)
- for the organization, employee retention
- again for the organization, congruence with organizational values, strategy or specific objectives
- profitability
- output
- utilization (e.g. percentage of time the equipment was in use)
- waiting time
- waste or rejects.

EASE OF MEASUREMENT

Bear in mind the ease of collecting data, when you select the indicators in your process. Unless you make it easy to collect the data, it may not happen; or if it does, you will simply be adding cost, resources and time to your process. By themselves, data add no value; so limit your checks to only those data that are essential to control and manage the process. 'Nice to know' is simply costing you more with no prospect of returns.

ACTIVITY 33

1 What indicators do you use to monitor the process you documented in Section 3, Activity 24?

2 Have you specified the standards or range of acceptable results for each?

3 Having documented your process, can you identify other indicators and metrics that may be appropriate?

When do you measure?

Process improvements of any kind require considerable investment of time and effort; you'll want to know what difference they make. Quantify what the process delivered **before** improvement and what the process delivered **after** improvement, and compare the two. If all other things are equal, then any change may be attributed to the improvement you have made.

The process is continually delivering outputs to your internal and external customers. You need to know on an **ongoing basis** that what you deliver meets or exceeds their requirements. If there are problems, you need to know the extent of them, how frequently they arose, and how they impacted on the customer, so that you can take action. Measurement is still the answer.

AT THE END

The detailed output specification you develop with your customer will be one yardstick for the **eventual output** at the end of your process. But checking results at the end provides little information about the individual activities within the process. What it does tell you may be too late. By then, you could have wasted considerable energy and resources on an unacceptable output – a typical effect of 'inspected in' quality.

If you're considering the refunds process of your organization, for example, measuring results at the end may tell you that the refund took one full month longer than promised, but it doesn't tell you why – whether the branch office used the wrong form and had to resubmit, or head office delayed the cheque request, or it got lost in the mail. It doesn't tell you how efficiently each of the individual activities was completed, or whether the right output was delivered at every stage.

DURING THE PROCESS

If you want to build in quality, you need 'windows' on the process to track the output as it moves through the process. Then you can identify where any problems creep in, and take action as soon as possible to correct them, so that you don't waste time and resources on outputs that are not up to scratch. Your process map from Section 3 – and any improvements or re-design since – may have revealed opportunities for these kinds of checks within individual activities, or on handovers between different individuals, teams or departments. Which are the activities that have greatest impact on effectiveness, efficiency or responsiveness? These are likely to offer the most productive opportunities for monitoring.

ACTIVITY 34

Take another look at the process map you drew in Section 3, Activity 24 and your answers to Activity 33.

1 How frequently do you measure your process against the indicators you have identified? (One-off, every year, every month, every day?)

Indicator **Frequency of measurement**

2 What opportunities can you see on your process chart for in-process monitoring?

Who measures?

Who does the measuring may seem obvious once you determine when and where you're going to measure the process. It makes sense to measure results as soon as possible after each critical activity; surely the best person to measure the results is whoever completes the task? But when your job depends on your people achieving certain standards, how far are you prepared to trust them to vet outputs for themselves? Clarifying the indicators, how they are to be measured, and the acceptable range, should lessen the risk. There is, however, a cautionary tale.

CASE STUDY

A manager was showing visitors round the site and introduced a process operative. 'This is Anna, our star operative. As you can see from this chart, 100 per cent of her sampled parts are within tolerances.' Impressed by this, the consultant asked to see her testing five random parts. Not one of the parts fell within acceptable tolerances. 'Oh,' she said, 'You'd be surprised how many I have to test sometimes, just to get five for the chart.'

So people need to understand the **purpose** of their self-checks, as well as what to do, when, and how.

ACTIVITY 35

Who could measure the relevant indicators you identified above? Who has the opportunity? What would they need to support their assessment and ensure accuracy and fairness.

Collecting and using the information

There are a wide range of methods for collecting and presenting data. For example, ticksheets, bar charts, Pareto Charts, line graphs and control charts. You will find references to further reading about these techniques in the Information Toolbox at the end of the workbook.

*By themselves, all the data in the world, even when analysed in the most sophisticated ways, accomplish nothing. In fact, data collection, data analysis and data storage, are activities that add no value **until the data are used to control, inform or improve a process.***

(Harrington, p. 194)[1]

The whole point of measuring, and gathering data, is to monitor process performance so that you can identify **where** action is required and **what** action may be most appropriate.

STANDARDS AND TARGETS

Once you know what results you actually get, you can decide what results you want. You can set **standards** and **targets**.

Standards

Standards are the **minimum** acceptable levels of performance to satisfy your customer or the organization. In effectiveness measures, these are likely to be the standards your customer specified for the outputs. In efficiency measures, you may find that you need to set your own standards, based on your records of past performance, and the levels of profit or throughput required to break even on the process. Alternatively, benchmarking may help you to specify appropriate standards.

Harrington[1] points out that half your work force will be 'below average'. The process, therefore, needs to be designed so that below average workers can deliver the outputs to minimum standards. If they can't, you may need to change your process so they can.

Targets

Targets are the **improvement goals** you set for the process. They are objectives designed to stretch, but also to reward – there's a sense of real achievement in hitting targets. Targets may involve delivering more (or better) with the same resources; or using fewer resources to deliver the same (or better).

If you don't have targets, the only goal you will have is to be perfect. If your only objective is never to make another error, each time you do make an error, you have failed, and that soon becomes unmotivating.

(Harrington, p. 182)[1]

ACTIVITY 36

- What standards are currently set for your process? Who sets them?

- What targets are currently set for the same indicators? Who sets them?

- What happens when you achieve them?

THE FEEDBACK SYSTEM

Taking measures is not just a one-off event. You'll need to know on an ongoing basis how your process is performing. So, having identified the key indicators, and the best method of collecting and presenting the data for interpretation, the next step is to **formalize** the data collection and graphing.

Set up a system that collects this data on a regular basis so that you can compare results with standards and targets. The system should specify exactly what should be checked, how frequently, and by whom – and what kinds of results should trigger action.

Once a system is in place, and responsibility is assigned for it, you won't have to start from scratch every time you want to collect this information.

The right information should automatically be collected and presented in the right way at the right time, to provide the feedback you need to decide what to do and when to do it. And the staff, time and resources for the data collection and feedback system can be anticipated and factored into your plans, schedules and budgets.

ACTIVITY 37

Use the form below to systematize your data collection and interpretation for your processes.

Details	**Process 1**	**Process 2**	**Process 3**	**Process 4**
Data to collect?				
How often?				
Who to collect?				
Report to whom?				
How to present?				
Who to generate?				
Standards set?				
Targets set?				
What triggers for action?				

Benchmarking

How do you know what targets to set? You may be able to specify targets based on 'best performance' currently achieved within the process. But – however stretching these targets are for the process itself – if they are lower than your competitors' targets, they're unlikely to bring competitive advantage.

Benchmarking involves comparing your process with best practice in similar processes elsewhere in the organization, in competitor organizations, in parallel but non-competing organizations, and/or in different industries using similar processes (see Figure 5.1).

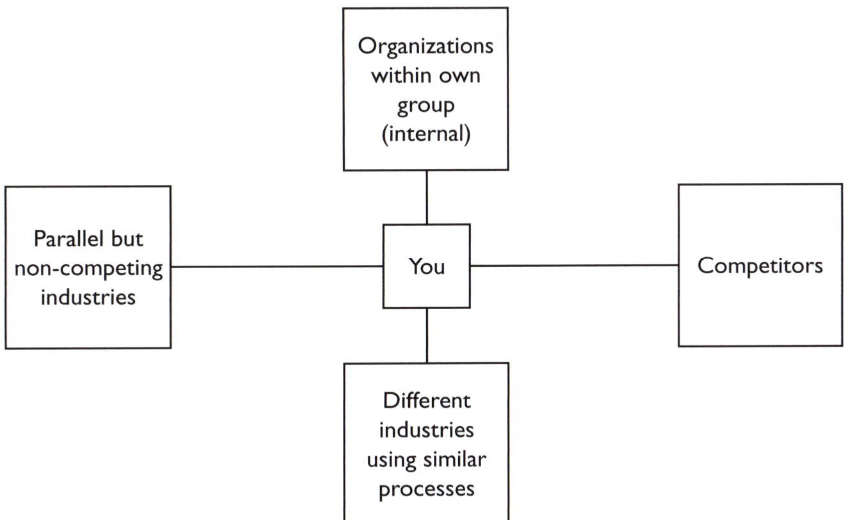

Figure 5.1 Who to benchmark

Because benchmarking shows what can be done, and gives everyone a chance to share ideas about their own work, it can be enormously motivating for the people involved. Where you cannot transplant the ideas directly, you may be able to modify or adapt them. Benchmarking can stimulate thinking about the process in new ways, and lead to more creative ideas for improvement. And it can lead to wider recognition for excellence within the process; even underperforming processes may have some excellent aspects.

HOW TO DO IT

The first task is to decide what you want to benchmark: select processes where you believe there is potential for improvement, or which consume most effort and resources. Document these processes and list the essential indicators – and current performance levels. You need to know your own processes thoroughly before you start to consider how others work. Identify benchmark comparators: this may be the most time consuming part of the process. Good places to start include benchmarking research bodies, trade associations and institutions, and suppliers and customers. Share your data with these comparators, and determine where differences arise, and why. (Do be careful when comparing figures – make sure you're comparing like with like.) Then, as with any measurement exercise, use the information to make a decision and take appropriate action.

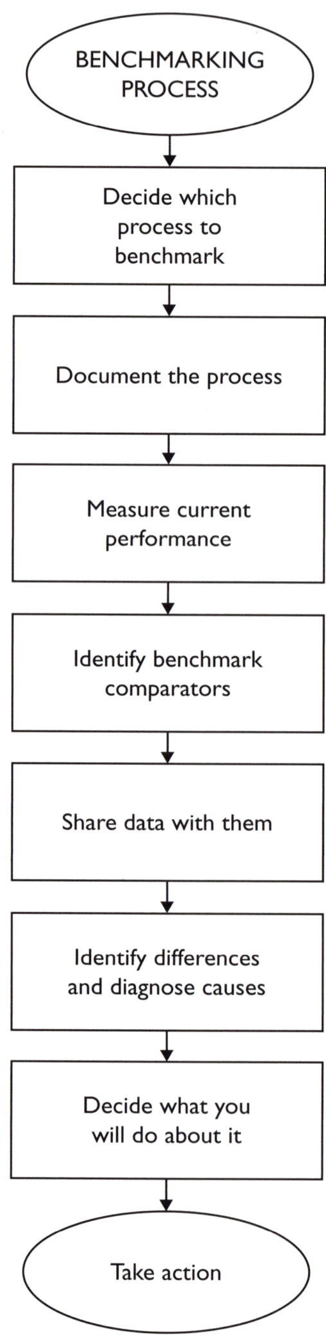

Figure 5.2 Benchmarking process

Table 5.1 shows the Chartered Management Institute's suggestions for successful benchmarking.

Table 5.1 Institute of Management checklist: a programme for benchmarking

Do	Don't
Ensure senior management support	Underestimate the need for willingness to change
Ensure it is a team activity	Be too ambitious at the start
Understand your own processes first	View benchmarking as a tool for short-term gains

TAKE YOUR TIME

This tour of benchmarking is necessarily brief. If you are seriously considering benchmarking (and it can be a powerful tool for key processes), we recommend that you invest some time finding out more about the techniques:

- Talk to organizations that are already benchmarking their processes.
- Read books or articles on the subject – such as *Practical Benchmarking – A manager's guide to creating a competitive advantage*, by Sarah Cook, published by Kogan Page (1995); or 'How to build a benchmarking team' by M.J. Spendolini, *Journal of Business Strategy*, vol. 14, no. 2, Mar/Apr, 1993, pp. 53–57.
- Contact the Benchmarking Council or the Benchmarking Centre.

ACTIVITY 38

- Which processes might benefit from benchmarking in your organization?

- Which organizations might offer useful benchmarking comparators?

- What might you be able to offer them?

One last word on the subject: benchmarking is a two-way deal. It's no good imagining you'll sweep in, pick your competitor's brains and steal their good ideas, and get clean away. They'll be looking for your ideas too: consider what you can offer them.

Learning summary

- If processes exist to enable the organization to achieve its objectives and deliver outputs to customers, the better you do this, the greater your competitive advantage. But you need **indicators** and **measures** to compare process performance; otherwise how will you know you're improving?
- For many organizations, the difficulty arises in **selecting** the indicators, or in **measuring** them. Select indicators that accurately correlate with the quality you want to measure – whether this is effectiveness, efficiency, or responsiveness. However, measurement alone will add no value to your process: so focus on essential measures only.
- It's no good measuring the output only at the end of the process; by then, you may have wasted considerable time and resources on an output that is not acceptable. For optimum control, there must be windows on the process that enable you to check outputs as the process flows through the organization.
- **Measurement** is best done as soon as possible after the activity; the best person to carry out the checks may be the person who completes the activity. However, this requires a degree of trust which may be lacking in the organization or in individual managers. There may be concerns about accuracy of test results which may make peer evaluation, or other arrangements, more appropriate.
- The purpose of gathering data is to inform decision-making and lead to more productive action.
- **Standards** are the minimum acceptable levels of performance in each indicator to satisfy the customer or the organization. **Targets** are improvement goals you set for the process. Both should help control and improve process results.
- **Data collection and analysis** is not a one-off; the process must be monitored and reviewed on an ongoing basis. The **feedback system** must be formalized so that the right information is automatically gathered and analysed at the right time to facilitate action planning.
- **Benchmarking** can help keep the organization in touch with best practice in the organization, in the process type, or in the industry, resulting in more challenging stretch targets and the sharing of innovative ideas. However, this can never be a 'quick fix'. Relationships of trust with competitors or other outside organizations take time to develop; and benchmarking partners will expect to learn something from you in return.

Into the workplace

You need to:

- identify quality checkpoints along your team's processes and select appropriate measures
- benchmark processes against similar processes elsewhere in the organization or in external organizations.

References

1 Harrington H. J. (1991) *Business Process Improvement*, McGraw-Hill

Section 6 Changing to a continuous improvement culture

Introduction

Making improvements is about continuous change. Nothing stands still as people pro-actively strive to make improvements. However, many people find it difficult to cope with change and changes in the workplace have to be managed sensitively.

In this section of the workbook, we consider what people contribute to the process of change and why managers may fail to actualize this potential. We review the factors that enable people to deliver process results: information, resources, incentives, skills training, intrinsic capacity, and motivation. Manipulating these factors may therefore help to enhance process performance. In the second half of the section, we explore the issues that the process approach may raise: conflicts of individual and organizational interests; changing roles and responsibilities (including the future of management); and the challenge to (or congruence with) corporate culture.

People matter

If process innovation is to succeed, the human side of change cannot be left to manage itself. Organizational and human resource issues are more central than technology issues to the behavioural changes that must occur within a process.

(Davenport, p. 96)[1]

Processes, systems or procedures cannot achieve anything on their own. They can all be replicated by your competitors. What distinguishes your service or product from your competitors' is the people who deliver it – their unique combination of knowledge, skills and attitudes and the collective culture of the organization as a whole. However, there may be a tendency to focus on the practical, technical elements of systems; and to pay too little attention to the human side. The introduction of change has to be managed carefully.

ACTIVITY 39

Why do you think people issues are often ignored? What steps can be taken to improve this?

FEEDBACK

This inattention to people may stem from the tradition of Taylorian management early this century, when operatives in predominantly mass production processes were manipulated almost as interchangeable factors of production. Tasks were broken down into the smallest possible chunks that required the least possible element of skill or personal judgement, in an effort to standardize production. The contribution of the individual to this mix was minimal, and consequently might be ignored with impunity.

This is no longer the case. More people are involved in service and knowledge-based industries where the contribution of the individual is the output for customers. In production environments, increasing automation and computerization mean that the remaining human tasks may be less routinized, and more concerned with identifying and handling exceptions. New organizational structures and increasing participation may push responsibility down the line. It is no longer enough simply to complete a given task; the individual is the prime value adder and output creator. The contribution of the individual is therefore central to organizational success.

EMOTIONAL TIMEBOMB?

Part of the hesitation in dealing with the human aspects of introducing changes may stem from discomfort in the face of human emotions, and a sense that people are more difficult to deal with and much less predictable than tasks or things.

Work may be a defining factor in our perceptions of our self and sense of self-worth. Work underwrites our life decisions and lifestyles – our homes, family and relationships, hobbies and holidays. We invest a lot of our time, energy, and creativity in it. It may be one way of giving meaning to life, if we feel that we are doing something worthwhile. Our behaviour at work may express our deepest values and beliefs. Work may validate the individual within a wider context; it may secure recognition and reward; it may also enhance status. So challenging or changing what people do (which is a fundamental precept of continuous improvement) may seem to challenge or threaten a whole way of life.

So people may feel a terrible sense of loss when faced with change in their work tasks. Elisabeth Kubler-Ross,[2] a writer and counsellor with considerable experience of dealing with loss and grief, suggests people move through phases:

- **denial** (This has nothing to do with me. We're doing all right; we don't need to change)
- **anger** (I've had it up to here with these new fads. This is asking too much. I've slogged my guts out and now you want more)
- **bargaining** (Well OK, so long as … Let's work out a compromise)
- **fear** (What if I'm not up to it? I don't know if I can cope)
- **resignation** (I guess if it's going to happen anyway, I'll have to go along with it).

Depending on their experiences, and the impact of the change, people may also experience:

- **hope** (So things will be better in future)
- **enthusiasm** (This is the best thing that's happened. Look what we can do now).

The phases aren't necessarily sequential; people may zig-zag between them, or start enthusiastic, and loop back through fear and anger when they realize just what's involved. They may feel some phases more than others, or even leap straight in at hope and enthusiasm. Everyone may be different.

'ACTING OUT' THE EMOTIONS

These emotions have a strong influence on how people actually behave at work: enthusiasm may lead to a missionary fervour; fear, anger, and sheer bewilderment may lead to almost subversive resistance.

ACTIVITY 40

1 Think back to a major organizational change you have experienced in the past. How did you feel about it, and how did you feel you were treated?

2 How will you use this experience to help you deal more effectively with the people involved in the process you manage?

Bringing people on board

You may spend a great deal of time thinking about how an improvement should be implemented. But not everyone has been with you at every step of the way. So you need to build ownership.

Share your thinking about how the process and procedures currently operate, the need for change and what you're trying to achieve. You may have lived with the reasons and the possibilities for the last 3 months; it'll take more than a single meeting or memo detailing the changes to bring people on board. Communication must be an ongoing process in itself. Give people time.

Management typically over-estimates the degree of co-operation it will get and under-estimates the transition costs. Among the by-products of significant restructuring are discontinuity, disorder and distraction – all of which tend to reduce productivity.

(Rosabeth Moss Kanter, Professor of Harvard Business School)

Where change is involved, shock or emotional reactions may prevent people from hearing what you say: they'll interpret it according to their own concerns. You say 'efficiency', and they hear redundancies. You say 'improve the process' and they hear a criticism of how they're doing it now. So think about where they are now, and tailor your message accordingly. Tell them what's in it for them. Acknowledge and address their underlying concerns. Repeat the message. Use different media, different words, different perspectives.

CASE STUDY

Fowler and Graves[3] (p. 49) cite one example of this. A defence supply company was earning a substantial proportion of its revenue from repair of its own equipment. Improving the quality of that equipment would therefore – in the eyes of the contracts manager – eliminate the guaranteed revenue this generated. So the contracts manager did everything in his power to resist the change – and nearly got himself sacked in the process.

Supporting people through change

Making an improvement must include dealing with everything people bring to the task – with their creativity and their feelings – as well as the logical and technological elements of the task. Only then can you begin to actualize their potential performance.

Most people come to work wanting to do a good job. Harrington[5] suggests that people deviate from a prescribed process or system because:

1. they **misunderstand** the procedures
2. they **don't know** the procedures
3. they don't understand **why** they should follow them
4. they find a **better** way of doing things
5. the procedure as documented is **too hard** to do
6. they don't have the **knowledge or skills**
7. they were **trained** to do it differently
8. someone **told** them to do it differently
9. they don't have the **tools**
10. they don't have the **time**.

INFORMATION	RESOURCES	INCENTIVES
Do they know: ■ what is involved? ■ what they are aiming for? ■ what is expected of them? ■ how their bits fit in? ■ how they're doing? ■ it's the truth and do they believe it?	Do they have: ■ the right structure or organization to achieve objectives? ■ the supplies, tools, equipment, time and staff to do it? ■ systems and standard procedures to help them do it? ■ access to support if they get stuck?	Do they receive: ■ appropriate rewards and recognition for doing things right? ■ no **penalties** for doing it right? ■ no rewards for doing it wrong?
KNOWLEDGE AND SKILLS	**CAPACITY**	**MOTIVATION**
Do they have the knowledge and skills: ■ to know what to do? ■ for process analysis and improvement? ■ to work effectively in a team? ■ to complete the technical and operational tasks in the process?	Do they have the: ■ self-confidence and emotional capacity? ■ intellectual capacity? ■ physical capacity?	Do they: ■ have autonomy? ■ actually WANT to do the tasks? ■ CARE about the results? ■ OWN the process?

Figure 6.1 Human performance model (adapted from Gilbert, T. F., *Human Competence*)[4]

GILBERT'S MODEL

There are no guaranteed tools to get this right; each manager must select and use the tactics that seem appropriate for the workers and the situation. However, one model proposed by the American T.F. Gilbert[4] and illustrated in Figure 6.1, may help to quantify the factors you need to consider, and offer possibilities to help you optimize the contribution people can make in your process.

ACTIVITY 41

1 Work through the six boxes in Gilbert's model, and check what factors are currently supporting the people who operate your process.

2 Identify any gaps, and consider how these could be remedied to help people operate the process more effectively, efficiently and responsively.

Motivation and incentives

Of all the factors in Gilbert's model, there may be most ambiguity around motivation and incentives. Managers may think that if they offer more incentives, people will be more motivated. But the two are quite different.

Incentives are what the organization offers; you may be able to change these. You can remove frustrations, or work people don't like; and enhance the rewards such as recognition, privilege, or pay. Get your incentives right and you may be able to persuade people to comply with the process. But you won't automatically tap into people's intimate knowledge of their own inputs and how the process works in practice; and people won't necessarily care enough to operate the process thoughtfully, or contribute their own ideas. You can buy someone's time, but that doesn't win their hearts.

Motivation is the natural drive or affinity an individual has towards (or away from) particular work or interests. When people are motivated to achieve something, they transcend compliance to access creativity, commitment and caring about how the process performs. Which, of course, is exactly what you need when you want to improve it.

How can you affect motivation? A 'pep' talk won't do the trick if it's something inherent in the individual. Research suggests that the following dimensions may influence motivation:

- **skill variety** (the range of skills involved in the tasks)
- **task identity** (the completeness of a task. For example, you may find building a complete car more satisfying than fitting a single part on any number of cars for the same period of time)
- **task significance** (the difference it makes)
- **autonomy** (control over the way the work is carried out)
- **feedback**.

So, if you want to enhance individual motivation, consider what scope there is to adjust one or more of these elements in the way that work is allocated.

ACTIVITY 42

Think back to a time when you were particularly demotivated at work (or at school or university). Which element in the above list was at fault, and how did you change the balance?

Conflict of interests?

So far, the assumption has been that if something is good for the process and the organization, it will ultimately be good for the individuals involved. This may not be the case.

The association of re-engineering with 'downsizing' and redundancies is not accidental; the majority of European efforts in this direction have been geared to cutting costs, and labour remains a major factor of costs. Although reducing staff may not be the prime objective of re-engineering, it may be a natural consequence of doing things more efficiently – achieving more with less.

IS MY JOB AT RISK?

Harrington highlights the dilemma:

Management cannot expect people to evaluate the business processes fairly and look for ways to improve them if it means that they or the person working beside them will be laid off. We believe that management should develop a no-layoff policy … Without this type of assurance, management cannot expect the full co-operation of the members of the performance improvement team or their management … people will hide waste to protect themselves, their friends, and their employees.

(Harrington, p. 53)[5]

While the logic of his premise is undisputable, the solution he suggests may seem more problematic.

PRODUCTION VERSUS CAPABILITY

Stephen Covey[6] highlights the need for balance between **production** (actual outputs or productivity) and production **capability** (the asset that produces the golden egg). In organizational terms, people are your production capability; cutting staff too drastically may compromise your ability to increase production when things pick up, or even to sustain existing levels of production. The result is a kind of corporate anorexia from which the organization gradually sinks into terminal decline.

(According to research conducted by the American Management Association) only 47 per cent of companies reporting workforce reductions since 1990 realised any increase in operating profits within a year following the reductions. Long-term, only 46 per cent reported increased profits. Only one-third … reported an increase in worker productivity.

David Stamps[7]

Where companies do show a gain in profit or productivity following a cut in staffing, they have generally expanded their training efforts at the same time – investing again in the production capability of the workforce.

ACTIVITY 43

What are the prospects of redundancy as a result of your process improvement effort? If relevant, what realistic assurances can you therefore offer your staff to allay fears about job security?

Roles and responsibilities

The process approach typically pushes power down the line to analyse, diagnose, and change the way work is done. The aim is to build autonomy, ownership and acceptance of any change, as well as increasing the quality of any change. However:

Don't expect people to change how they behave unless you change what they do; that is, their work must be designed to allow them to act differently.

(Champy, p. 110)[8]

There are implications in this for everyone concerned.

EMPOWERING OR DUMPING?

Bear in mind that not everyone wants increased responsibility for processes. It's convenient to be told what to do – less taxing, less tiring – and there's always someone else to blame if anything goes wrong. Besides, they're not paid for the responsibility ... There is a fine line between empowerment and being 'dumped on' and the main difference lies in how it's perceived by the individual.

ACTIVITY 44

1 Think back to a time when you were obliged to take responsibility for something you didn't want to do.

2 How did you feel about this?

3 And how did you deal with it?

4 What might have helped you come to terms with the responsibility?

FEEDBACK

You may have found that support and encouragement from your manager gave you confidence and the will to complete the task. Rewards or personal recognition may have gone some way to compensate for the effort required.

TEAM POWER

Empowered teams can produce extraordinary results, much greater than the sum of their individual parts. However:

Teams and workgroups have a shady side ... They can, for example, waste the time and energy of members rather than use them well. They can enforce norms of low rather than high productivity. They sometimes make notoriously bad decisions. Patterns of destructive conflict can arise, both within and between groups. And groups can exploit, stress and frustrate their members – sometimes all at the same time.

J. Richard Hackman[9]

ACTIVITY 45

1 How strong is the team identity among your team, and how does it manifest itself?

2 How might you reduce the risk of:
- dissipation of time and energies?
- norms of low productivity and a rejection of 'rate-busting'?
- destructive competition and conflict?

WHERE DOES THIS LEAVE THE MANAGER?

The internal power shift implicit in passing responsibility down the line may leave the manager in a quandary, too. If teams are responsible for satisfying their customers' needs, deciding where action is required and agreeing that action, what is left for managers to do?

For us managers, nothing seems sure any more, neither our professional know-how nor our career paths – and certainly not our job security … Management has joined the ranks of the dangerous professions.

(Champy, pp. 6–7)[8]

Champy goes on to articulate the new 'ordeal of management':

- nothing is simple any more …
- whatever we do is not enough …
- everything is in question …
- everyone must change …

Managers are not exempt from the emotional responses to loss we considered earlier.

When teams take on more responsibility, managers have the opportunity to move into a more facilitating and coaching role. This involves a change of style and tasks they may find foreign or difficult. Managers may lose the direct contact with the customer and the work that brought them personal satisfaction and promotion in the first place. And what managers contribute – which consolidates their own sense of self-worth and achievement – becomes harder to quantify. The Chinese say that the sign of a good leader is that when his people accomplish their goal, they say 'We did it ourselves'. But it's hard to forgo recognition for your efforts.

Champy points out that management resistance alone may be enough to scupper the process changes:

The three vice presidents ... at a major computer company were thrilled that re-engineered work processes promised to cut product introduction time in half, raise customer retention rates by 20 per cent, and slice 30 per cent from administrative costs in their areas. They weren't thrilled enough, however, to willingly give up control of their fiefdoms and collaborate. Result: the re-engineering effort died a year after its inception.

(Champy, p. 5)[8]

So don't forget yourself when you work through Gilbert's model.

ACTIVITY 46

Run through Gilbert's model and identify what YOU need to enable you to fulfil the new role and responsibilities implicit in the process approach.

Cultural congruence

Process improvements may present another dilemma for individuals and the organization as a whole. On the one hand, the aim is to challenge and change the way things are done, which may have a far-reaching impact on how people relate to each other and the way the organization operates. On the other hand, change is unlikely to take root where it is incompatible with established corporate culture – 'the way we do things round here'.

You may be familiar with the experience of coming back from a really stimulating and thought-provoking course, and wanting to put what you've learned into action, only to be squashed back into old moulds by the sheer force of cultural norms. This kind of chicken-and-egg situation may seem intractable, but there are precedents and possibilities.

For successful change:

- Secure **top management commitment** to the changes – not just verbal support, but real modelling of what they mean for people day to day. If the process approach is so important, why aren't the top team using it to deliver their outputs – formulating strategy, values, vision?
- **Involve the people** who will implement any changes, to build ownership.
- Create a compelling **vision** of how things will be – preferably a shared vision, in which people feel they have a stake.
- Emphasize where there is **continuity** – how the approach will align with the underlying values of the organization:

We have to provide something for people to hang onto, something that doesn't change.
(Champy, p. 54)[8]

- Build '**pockets**' of the new way of doing things (self-sustaining teams). Evidence suggests that much change originates on the periphery of the organization, and only migrates to the centre when it is proven and accepted. You won't convert everyone overnight; but once you have a few teams delivering real results, this may stimulate interest and prepare the ground, building critical mass.
- Give people **time**: All the evidence suggest that a major cultural change may take anything from 2 to 5 years. Two years is probably the minimum for a major process re-design or re-engineering. And once the change is in place, no matter how beneficial, it will still take people time to build competence in the new way of doing things, and make the process work up to its full potential.
- **Celebrate successes**: Give people plenty of feedback so they know how they're doing and what's working.

Learning summary

- When managing and improving processes, there may be a tendency to focus more on the technical aspects of processes rather than on people.
- Part of the reason may be discomfort in the face of the emotional disturbance that may be occasioned by any change. Unless you bring people on board, resistance may prove destructive.
- **Gilbert's model** is a reminder of the factors that managers may be able to influence in order to help people perform better:
  - information
  - resources
  - incentives
  - skills and knowledge (training)
  - capacity
  - motivation.
- **Motivation** is the key to accessing creativity and commitment; the degree of variety, identity, significance, autonomy and feedback inherent in the work may determine individual motivation.
- Improving processes may lead to a conflict of interests as people are expected to contribute to improvements that may ultimately make them redundant. Reducing staffing levels may also compromise production capability and contribute to a kind of corporate anorexia that jeopardizes the future existence of the organization.
- **Roles and responsibilities** necessarily change when processes are improved. But not everyone will welcome the empowerment and responsibility entailed. **Team structure** alone is not sufficient to ensure productive teamworking; managers must be aware of the possible risks, and take action to minimize these. At the same time, managers must be prepared to relinquish their old roles and adopt a more facilitating role.
- The process approach may also pose a dilemma for the organization: on the one hand, it seeks to challenge the way things are done; on the other, change is unlikely to take root where it is incompatible with corporate culture.

Into the workplace

You need to:

- consider the effect of change on your team members
- use techniques which will help team members to accept change and improve performance.

References

1 Davenport, T. H. (1993) *Process Innovation: re-engineering work through information technology*, Harvard Business School Press

2 Kubler–Ross, E. (1997) *On Death and Dying*, Scribner Book Company

3 Fowler, E. and Graves, P. (1995) *Managing of Effective Operation*, Institute of Management, Butterworth-Heinemann

4 Gilbert, T. F. (1978) *Human Competence*, McGraw-Hill

5 Harrington, H. J. (1991) *Business Process Improvement*, McGraw-Hill

6 Covey, S. R. (1992) *The Seven Habits of Highly Effective People*, Simon & Shuster

7 Stamps, D. (1996) Corporate anorexia, *Training*, February, pp. 24–30

8 Champy, J. (1995) *Re-engineering Management*, Harper Collins

9 Hackman, R. (1987) The Design of Work Teams, In (Lorsch, J., ed.) *Handbook of Organizational Behaviour*, cited in Davenport, 1993

Section 7 Continually improving health and safety

Introduction

Managing health and safety effectively requires a culture of striving for continuous improvement. It involves everyone taking responsibility to integrate and improve health and safety practices. It's a key management issue and managers need to be able to take a:

- **strategic** approach which looks at how, in the long term, the organization should be managing health and safety
- **pro-active** approach which looks at how health and safety matters can be managed effectively on a day-to-day basis
- **personal** approach which looks at how managers can, through their individual actions and responses, take a measure of personal responsibility for promoting and ensuring health and safety throughout the organization.

In this final section of the workbook we'll be looking at these three approaches to managing and implementing sound health and safety practices at work.

A strategic approach to health and safety

The main purposes of health and safety laws and regulations are to ensure that people have a safe and healthy working environment and that, as far as possible, accidents can be prevented. An accident can reasonably be described as 'an event that results in harm or damage to people or property or causes loss or disruption to process or procedures'.

The main current legislation is:

- Management of Health and Safety at Work Regulations 1992
- Workplace (Health, Safety and Welfare) Regulations 1992 (often referred to as the Workplace Regulations)
- Manual Handling Operations Regulations 1992
- Health and Safety (Display Screen Equipment) Regulations 1992
- Personal Protective Equipment at Work Regulations 1992
- Control of Substances Hazardous to Health (1988)
- Factories Act 1961 (since completely superseded by the 1992 Regulations – see below)
- Offices, Shops and Railway Premises Act 1963.

Under this legislation employers have a legal duty of care towards their employees, customers, suppliers and visitors. In practice, this means that employers are required to provide a safe and healthy working environment, and also make sure that the services they provide or the products they make are safe.

Effective health and safety – safe workplace, safe working practices, safe equipment and so on – has to be influenced top-down throughout the organization. In other words, once the staff know what is required of them it is their responsibility to do it, but it has to be the responsibility of senior management to develop health and safety policies and programmes, and make sure that these are effective.

The nine key steps for senior management, when creating a health and safety management programme are:

1. **analyse** the premises and working practices and identify the potential problems
2. **develop** health and safety policies and procedures
3. **organize** health and safety personnel and allocate individual responsibilities
4. **arrange** appropriate training
5. **devise** appropriate documentation
6. **implement** policies and procedures
7. **undertake** inspections and audits
8. **evaluate** performance
9. **make** changes and improvements, where necessary.

We'll look at each of these steps.

1 ANALYSING THE PREMISES AND WORKING PRACTICES AND IDENTIFYING THE POTENTIAL PROBLEMS

This step involves taking an in-depth look at every part of the building to make sure that it is safe. This includes everything from the structure and fabric of the building right down to identifying torn carpeting, spaghetti-junctions of electric cable, boxes of stationery dumped in the hallway, step ladders draped against the exit door, fire extinguishers that don't work and first-aid boxes that contain nothing more than two safety pins and an out-of-date sticking plaster.

It also means making sure that every single item of equipment (in the offices, warehouse, factory floor and on the road) is safe to use and regularly checked and serviced by someone who is suitably qualified and trained to do the checking. This includes ensuring that old, out-of-date and possibly unsafe plant, machinery and equipment is replaced with new (and possibly expensive) alternatives. Health and Safety law is not interested in cash-flow problems or impressed by comments like 'I was waiting to get the latest model which comes on the market next year.' If someone is harmed at work by unsafe equipment, then the employer is responsible.

It also includes making sure that everything from the layout of the building to the way in which production processes are organized and arranged should be safe for people. So, for example, it could be argued that it is unsafe to have the main reception desk sited right next to the ornamental fountain – on the basis that water and electricity (needed for the computer) are not a safe combination. It would be expected that a laboratory process involving radiation or acid or bacteria should be shielded from the rest of the building, and it would be reasonable to ensure that someone who regularly moves trays of hot material should not be expected to walk between two rows of desks where people are writing reports and making telephone calls.

And it also means that no one should be at risk of hurting themselves at work because they have to carry or move something which is too heavy, too large or toxic. This is not just obviously heavy objects like crates and pallets, but also smaller items such as printers and boxes of photocopying paper.

So this first stage of analysis involves identifying all of the potential risks, plus all the health and safety equipment and peripheral items needed. These might include anything from trolleys for moving heavy items through to protective clothing; fire extinguishers through to 'Exit' and 'No Smoking' signs.

Risk assessment involves:

- A careful examination of what, in your work, could cause people harm (i.e. the hazards)
- Weighing up the risk (i.e. the chances, great or small, that someone will be harmed by the hazard)
- Deciding whether you have taken enough precautions (or should do more to prevent harm).

2 DEVELOPING HEALTH AND SAFETY POLICIES AND PROCEDURES

This involves developing the procedures to be carried out in respect of:

- accident handling, investigation, reporting and documentation
- fire prevention and fire handling
- carrying out checks and inspections on the company's buildings, plant, equipment and machinery
- carrying out checks and inspections on health and safety equipment such as fire extinguishers, first-aid boxes, goggles, footwear and so on
- preventing and, where necessary, monitoring potentially harmful emissions from working practices
- monitoring good housekeeping practices such as storage facilities, waste disposal, safe use of machinery, electricity and gas
- ensuring that all health and safety matters are up to date and comply with current legislation.

3 ORGANIZING HEALTH AND SAFETY PERSONNEL AND ALLOCATING INDIVIDUAL RESPONSIBILITIES

Once you are clear about the procedures you need to adopt, you then need to identify the people who will be responsible for making sure that the procedures are actually carried out. (In any company with more than five employees, a manager must be appointed and trained as the company's Safety Representative.) The number of people and their individual responsibilities will depend on the type and size of the organization. Two possible structures are shown in Figures 7.1 and 7.2.

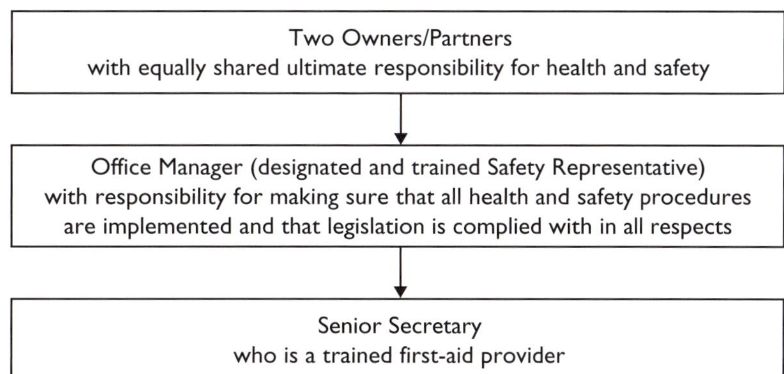

Figure 7.1 Health and safety structure for a small service company employing eight people

4 ARRANGING APPROPRIATE TRAINING

Everyone in the company, from the Managing Director through to the person responsible for taking care of the dish-washing machine in the canteen kitchen, must have adequate and appropriate health and safety training. This should include training in:

- hazard identification and reporting
- accident, illness, fire and explosion prevention and reporting
- building evacuation, including location of exits, entrances and fire extinguishers; escape routes and procedures
- safe working practices, including hygiene and good housekeeping
- safe operation of plant, machinery and equipment, including use of protective clothing and equipment, and the servicing and maintenance schedules for machinery
- safe handling of substances hazardous to health
- first-aid procedures and obtaining medical assistance, including location of first-aid boxes, first-aid room and first-aid personnel
- names and locations of health and safety officers, representatives and other trained personnel.

Everyone should know which machines or equipment they are, and are not, allowed to use. **Everyone** should be adequately trained to use their permitted machinery and equipment. This applies not only to recognized potentially dangerous items like fork-lift trucks, hand saws and drills, but also to items like electric staplers, photocopy machines, computers and even craft knives. If an employee injures themselves and truthfully says 'I was never told I had to take the plug out before I put my hand in it' it is the employer's responsibility. The key point here is that people should know what to do and how to do it, both to prevent accidents and problems, and to deal with accidents or problems when they occur.

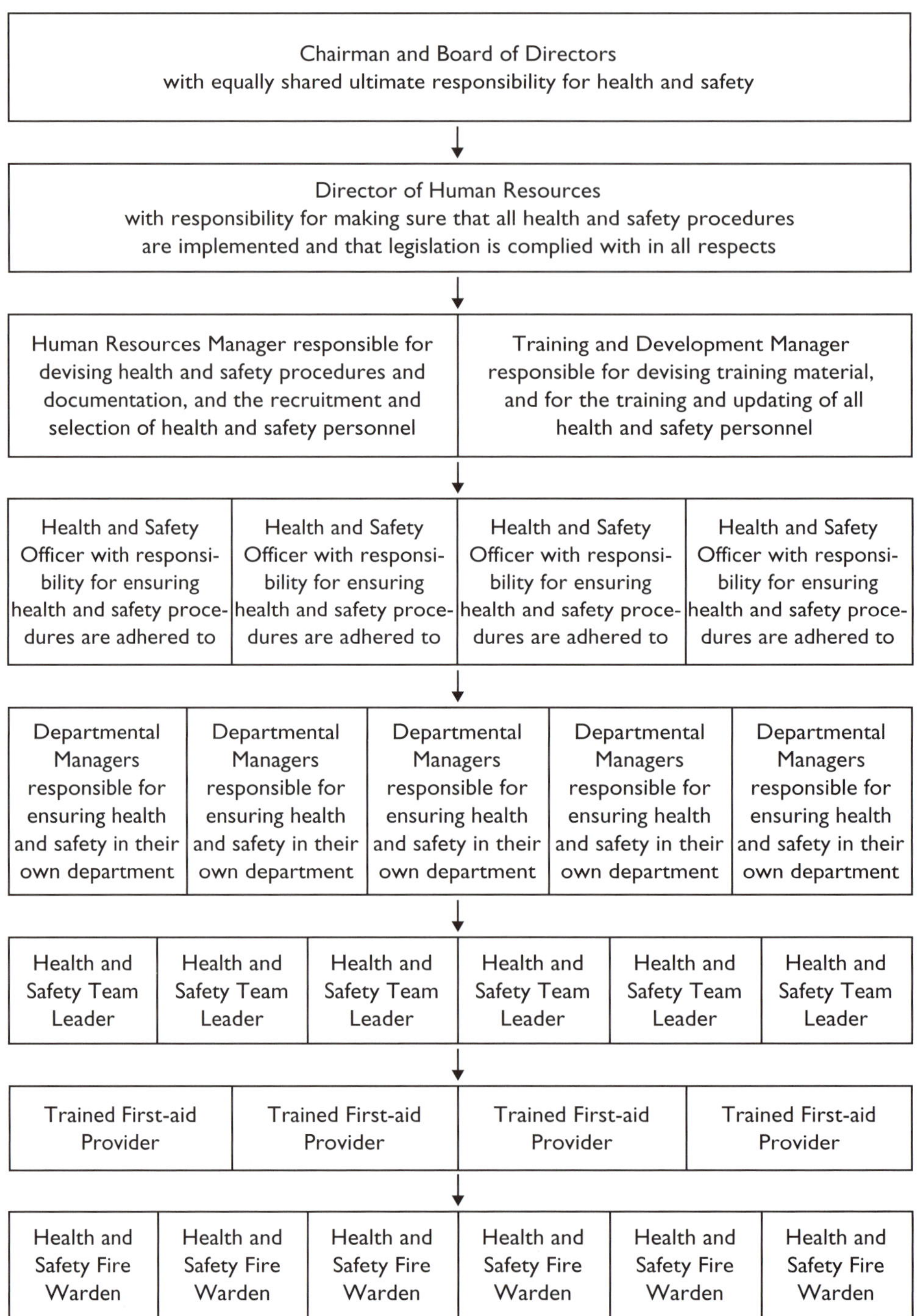

Figure 7.2 Health and safety structure for a large manufacturing company employing 350 people

5 DEVISING APPROPRIATE DOCUMENTATION

Health and safety documentation includes:

- information packs for staff (including updates when new legislation appears)
- accident report, investigation and conclusion forms
- equipment inspection and maintenance forms
- first-aid treatment and patient progress forms
- fire drill forms
- health and safety audit forms
- health and safety statistic forms (detailing the number of accidents, fires and so on).

6 IMPLEMENTING POLICIES AND PROCEDURES

It isn't the end of the story when all the policies, procedures and documentation are in place, and everyone has had the training. This is when people – managers, health and safety officers, team leaders – have to make sure that they drive the programme through and that staff are sticking to the procedures, and the procedures work in the way they were intended to work.

As a manager, no matter what your key objectives are, or what your particular specialism or area of interest, health and safety has to be high on your agenda. The legislation which governs and controls health and safety in the UK is very clear that it is the **employer's responsibility** to make sure the staff are working in a healthy and safe environment. This means that, as part of the management team, you have to keep your eye on the ball and never dismiss any aspect of health and safety as something that is just the 'flavour of the month' or 'an intrusion on the real business we're here for'. Specifically, if you see something which needs attention (even if it is a minor problem like a pile of rubbish, or a Fire Exit sign that is hanging off the wall), don't walk by because you are too busy dealing with profit and loss, or productivity or market share. No company wants to have staff injuries or deaths on its conscience, and no company can afford the bad press which always accompanies a bad safety record. So, from both an ethical and a purely commercial point of view, good health and safety awareness and practices make sound business sense.

7 UNDERTAKING INSPECTIONS AND AUDITS

Safety inspections and audits play a key role in raising health and safety awareness within an organization. They also ensure that all the equipment, systems and procedures are properly maintained and servicing is recorded.

8 EVALUATING PERFORMANCE

By looking at the results of the inspections and audits you can see, from the figures, whether or not the organization's health and safety performance is adequate, good or outstanding.

9 MAKING CHANGES AND IMPROVEMENTS, WHERE NECESSARY

Depending on the evaluation of performance it may be necessary to make changes and improvements. These changes may include:

- implementing additional procedures
- changing existing procedures or documentation
- changing some elements of the health and safety training programme
- appointing additional staff to take responsibility for health and safety.

The next activity will give you an opportunity to consider some of these issues.

ACTIVITY 47

Think about the way in which health and safety is managed and implemented within your own organization. See if you can identify, for each of the topics listed below, improvements or changes which would be of benefit to both the company and the employees.

1 Analysis of the premises and working practices, and identification of potential problems.
How, in your opinion, could this process be improved?

2 Development of health and safety procedures.
Are there any procedures which could be improved? How could these improvements be implemented?

3 Organization of health and safety personnel, and allocation of individual responsibilities.
Does the current health and safety personnel structure work? Is the way in which responsibilities are allocated effective and appropriate? Do you have any suggestions for improvement?

4 Appropriate training.
Is current health and safety training appropriate and sufficient for everyone? Could you suggest how training might be improved?

5 Appropriate documentation.
Is the current documentation straightforward and easy to use? What changes could you suggest for improvement?

6 Implementation of policies and procedures.
Are there any ways in which health and safety procedures in your organization could be sharpened up and improved?

7 Inspections and audits.
Are inspections and audits undertaken regularly, and thoroughly? How might these be improved?

8 Evaluation of performance.
How is the evaluation of performance undertaken, and who is responsible? Do you have any suggestions for improvement?

9 Making changes and improvements.
Is your organization responsive to the evaluation results? Are changes and improvements actually carried out, when necessary? What would you do to improve the process?

A pro-active approach to health and safety

Every organization has to make sure that it is complying with the legal and regulatory health and safety requirements. This compliance has to be consistent, appropriate and monitored on a daily or even hourly basis (where, say, excessive amounts of waste material are generated).

Taking a pro-active approach to health and safety means that, as a manager, working for any kind of organization, anywhere in the UK, you need to know both the law and the regulations, so you can:

- judge whether or not the law and the regulations are being complied with, and
- know what to do to put things right, when necessary.

WORKPLACE REGULATIONS

The 1992 Workplace Regulations are a key item of European legislation and relevant to most workplaces. The main health and safety issues covered by the 1992 Workplace Regulations (in alphabetical order, **not** in order of importance) are:

- cleanliness and waste
- conditions of floors or traffic routes
- drinking water
- escalators and moving walkways
- facilities for storing and changing clothes
- falls or falling objects
- indoor temperatures
- lighting
- maintenance of equipment and systems
- rest period accommodation and meal facilities
- room dimensions and space
- sanitary and washing facilities
- seating and workstations
- ventilation
- windows, gates, walls and doors.

COSHH

Under the Control of Substances Hazardous to Health (COSHH) Regulations 1988 organizations are required to:

- identify and assess the risks to health
- decide on the necessary precautions
- control or prevent the risks
- ensure the control measures are continuously implemented
- monitor the exposure to risk and, where necessary, the health of employees
- ensure that employees are informed of the risks, and trained to avoid and prevent them.

To identify substances hazardous to health you can check Part IA1 of the Approved List, Classification, Packaging and Labelling of Dangerous Substances Regulations 1984. Any substances listed there as very toxic, toxic, corrosive, harmful or irritant are covered by the COSHH regulations.

Aside from specific substances (corrosives, acids, solvents, etc.) that are used for a specific purpose, it is also useful to think about production processes to identify whether staff might be at risk from dust, fumes or residues. It is worth noting that asbestos, lead and radio-active materials all have their own specific handling regulations which must be complied with.

HEALTH AND SAFETY AT WORK ACT 1974

The Health and Safety at Work Act (HASAWA) 1974 is the **key** piece of legislation which applies, in its entirety, to **every** company in the UK. The next activity will give you an opportunity to consider what this really means, in practical terms.

ACTIVITY 48

Under the HASAWA:

1 For whose health and safety is an employer responsible?

2 For whose health and safety is an employee responsible?

FEEDBACK

Under HASAWA, **employers** are responsible for the health and safety of:

- Employees and other workers, whether they are:
  - full time or part time
  - permanent, temporary or casual
  - on work experience from school or college
  - attending the workplace as part of a Government training scheme
- Visitors
  - on-site as a subcontractor
  - visiting or using the premises for any purpose
  - using the firm's equipment for any purpose
- Customers buying or using products made, or services supplied, by the organization
- Members of the general public, particularly those living in the local neighbourhood near to the workplace who might be affected by noise, toxic emissions and so on.

Basically, this list covers just about **anyone** who works at, lives near, or visits the workplace, for whatever reason.

Under Section 7(a) of HASAWA, **employees'** health and safety responsibilities are defined as:

It shall be the duty of every employee while at work to take reasonable care for the health and safety of himself and of other persons who may be affected by his acts or omissions at work.

In practice, this means that each employee is responsible for their own health and safety, and the health and safety of everyone who works at or visits the workplace premises.

FINANCIAL IMPLICATIONS

As we said earlier, ethics dictate that companies should comply with the legislation. In addition, compliance is good business practice because the financial implications of health and safety problems can be considerable.

ACTIVITY 49

For the purposes of this activity imagine that, in your organization, two employees, whilst operating machinery, are involved in a serious accident. Both employees are hospitalized and need to be off work for at least 3 months each. List four of the likely financial costs your company would have to meet as a result of the accident.

1

2

3

4

FEEDBACK

The financial implications of a serious accident involving two employees could include the cost of:

- sickness benefit and/or compensation for the individuals involved in the accident
- additional payments to replacement staff – agency people or overtime payments to existing employees
- lost production or reduced service levels
- repair or replacement of damaged or faulty machinery
- accident investigation and reporting procedures
- management meetings to discuss future accident prevention measures to be implemented
- increased premium to insurance company (although research figures show that over 90 per cent of the financial costs of a workplace accident are uninsured)
- bad press, possibly accompanied by loss of consumer and shareholder confidence, maybe resulting in:
  - loss of market share
  - reduction in share prices
  - loss of future investment or loan facilities.

Apart from accidents, unsafe or unacceptable working practices can also cause considerable financial loss. This has been shown to be the case during the adverse publicity surrounding the BSE 'Mad Cow' controversy. Some companies immediately swung into action to reassure the public that their working practices were being totally overhauled and updated. For those companies public confidence remained strong, and they retained their market share. Other companies decided that it was 'a fuss about nothing which would quickly blow over'. UK consumers retaliated by reducing their purchases of British beef and disassociating themselves from companies which had not strictly followed the health and safety guidelines relating to slaughter and carcass stripping. The public voted with their feet, and their money.

There would also be other equally important costs which may not necessarily be financial. These could include:

- loss of employee confidence
- reduction in employee motivation and morale, possibly accompanied by lowered productivity or quality standards.

The key point here is that once the strategic, long-term planning has been done, and all the staff, systems and procedures are in place, every company must take a pro-active approach to health and safety. This means keeping up to date with, and conforming to, the legislation; regularly updating and improving staff training; constantly monitoring and persistently looking at ways in which continuous health and safety improvements can be made. Health and safety should never be just a paper exercise. Get it wrong, and you put families, careers, even lives at risk.

A personal approach to health and safety

As a manager, you have health and safety responsibilities towards:

- your employer
- your colleagues
- your team
- anyone and everyone who visits your company's premises, or who uses your company's products or services
- yourself.

ACTIVITY 50

How can you, at a personal level, make a practical contribution to health and safety at work? List three things you can do to demonstrate your personal commitment to health and safety.

1

2

3

FEEDBACK

As a manager, you are a role model for excellence. In matters of health and safety (and most other things too) you have to lead from the front and set a good example.

CASE STUDY

David, an accountant, and member of his company's senior management team, describes how he learned the hard way about example setting:

'We were in Scotland in the middle of winter and I'd spent three hours on-site talking to people. As you can imagine, I was absolutely frozen. I was on my way back to my car and, to be honest, all I could think about was whether or not I was ever going to be able to defrost my feet. Then I realized I'd forgotten to give a really important instruction to the site foreman ... so I popped back, just wanting to get the whole thing over with as quickly as possible. I didn't call back into the main building for the protective gear ... well, I was only going to be there for a minute, wasn't I? Long story cut short ... there was a problem with one of the cranes and I missed instant death by about 2 cm. No one congratulated me on living to tell the tale ... but there was a great deal of bad feeling because I was on-site without a hard hat. That story ran and ran ... and I was very disadvantaged by it. I couldn't take anyone to task about health and safety at work ... because everyone felt that if I had no respect for the rules, why should they bother?'

The practical things you can do to demonstrate personal commitment to health and safety are:

- Lead from the front
  - observe the rules and regulations at all times
  - take appropriate action when you see other people who are not observing the rules. Don't just walk past and turn a blind eye
  - listen carefully to problems, concerns and suggestions for improvement, and then take appropriate action
  - say nothing and do nothing **ever** which might give people the impression that you do not regard health and safety as a key issue, of paramount importance.
- Check and monitor, constantly
  - walk the job and see for yourself whether or not everything is in order; whether or not people are observing health and safety requirements
  - always make it known that you are serious about the topic and that you expect other people to be serious, too.

Learning summary

- A **strategic approach** involves looking at how the organization should be managing health and safety in the long term
- A **pro-active approach** involves looking at how health and safety can be managed on a day-to-day basis
- A **personal approach** involves taking personal responsibility for ensuring the promotion and observance of health and safety practices and procedures
- The nine key steps for creating a health and safety management programme are:
  1. analyse the situation and identify potential problems
  2. develop policies and procedures
  3. organize personnel and allocate responsibilities
  4. arrange training
  5. devise documentation
  6. implement systems, policies and procedures
  7. undertake inspections and audits
  8. evaluate performance
  9. make any necessary changes.
- The main pieces of legislation which you, as a manager, need to be familiar with are:
  - The Management of Health and Safety at Work Regulations 1992
  - Workplace (Health, Safety and Welfare) Regulations 1992
  - Control of Substances Hazardous to Health Regulations 1988 (COSHH)
  - Health and Safety at Work, etc. Act 1974 (HASAWA).

- As a manager you can demonstrate personal commitment to health and safety by:
  - observing the rules **all the time**
  - taking action when you see others who are not observing the rules
  - listening carefully to health and safety concerns – and taking action to put things right
  - walking the job and seeing for yourself what is going on
  - letting everyone know that you are serious about health and safety – and that you expect people to follow the rules.

Into the workplace

You need to:

- Implement and practically support health and safety legal requirements.

Appendix A The quality gurus

Since its early beginnings in the 1950s, quality improvement or total quality management has given rise to various people whose beliefs, ideologies and theories have been proven to be successful in turning below-average companies into successful businesses, mediocre companies into excellent companies, and good companies into the world's best. These people have been termed 'gurus' in recognition of their expertise.

Each of the 'gurus' has his own theory of how a total culture or programme may be introduced and sustained. Whilst there are obvious similarities in their approaches there are also differences which make each of the gurus distinctive.

It is important to note that the theories which helped to change post-war Japan did not come from Japan itself, but from the minds of Americans, in particular Dr W. Edwards Deming and Dr Joseph Moses Juran.

Today, there are many quality and total quality consultants but only a handful of recognized gurus. This handful includes Deming, Juran, Crosby and Ishikawa and they are probably the most renowned and revered of all Quality experts.

This appendix will look briefly at some of these gurus.

Dr W. Edwards Deming

Deming was a hero in Japan for some thirty years before he was given recognition in his homeland – the USA. This happened in June 1980 when he broadcast on NBC on the now famous subject 'if the Japanese can ... why can't we?'

Deming's theory centres around the belief that whilst quality is everyone's job, management must lead the effort, independent of the size of the organization or sector of the market. He is also an enthusiastic campaigner for training and believes that there can be no substitute for knowledge. This is clearly reflected in his classic 14 points for industrial revival and transformation.

DEMING'S 14 POINTS

1. Create constancy of purpose
2. Adopt a new philosophy
3. Cease dependence on inspection
4. Stop awarding business on price
5. Improve constantly and forever the system of production and service
6. Institute training on the job
7. Institute leadership
8. Drive out fear
9. Break down inter-departmental barriers
10. Eliminate slogans, exhortations and numerical targets
11. Eliminate quotas or work standards and management by objectives or numerical goods
12. Allow pride of workmanship
13. Institute a vigorous education and self-improvement programme
14. Put everyone in the company to work to achieve the transformation.

The 14 points are undoubtedly fine aims or goals. However, it is widely regarded that Deming provides no tools to achieve these goals. They in fact become more of a philosophy than a management practice.

Deming also talks about 'deadly diseases' and 'obstacles' which prevent organizations from performing at the highest levels. These include:

- violation of the 14 points
- emphasis on short-term profits
- mobility of management
- performance evaluation

and other parameters such as:

- motivation
- education
- reliance on standards
- use of technology.

No discussion of Deming, no matter how brief, would be complete without mention of the Deming cycle. This cycle, also known as the PDCA (plan, do, check, act) cycle, may be used as a helpful procedure for making improvements.

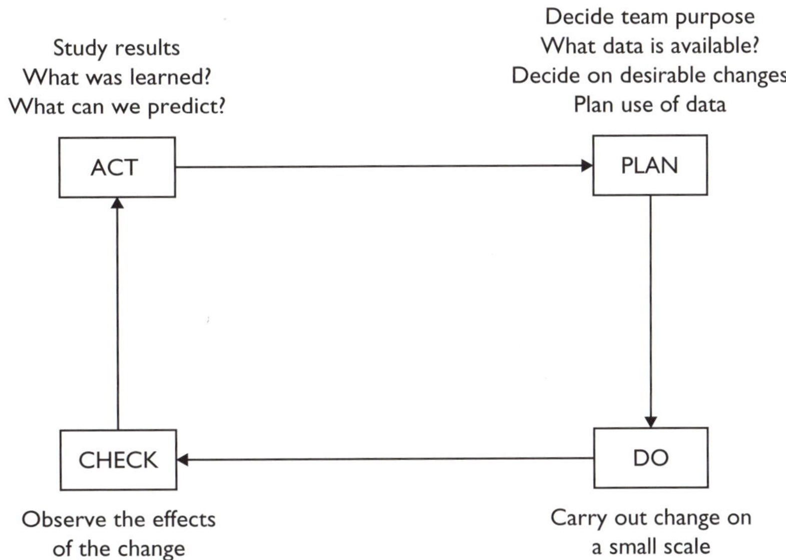

Figure A1 Deming's PDCA cycle

Joseph Moses Juran

Juran was a pioneer of quality education in Japan and like Deming remained relatively unknown in the USA until the 1980s. His research has shown that over 80 per cent of quality defects are management controllable and, therefore, it is management that needs to change.

Juran bases this path to success on the quality trilogy of **quality planning, quality control** and **quality improvement.**

Proper quality planning results in a process which is capable of meeting quality goals under operating conditions.

THE PLANNING ROAD MAP

1. Identify customers
2. Determine the needs of the customers
3. Translate those needs into the organization's language
4. Develop a product to meet those needs
5. Optimize the product features to meet organizational needs as well as customer needs
6. Develop a process capable of producing the product
7. Optimize the process
8. Prove the process under operating conditions
9. Transfer the process to operations.

Juran sees quality control resulting in the conduct of operations in accordance with the quality plan. Quality improvement ensures that the conduct of operations achieves a quality level in excess of the planned performance.

All three programmes are dependent on people with specialist skills and knowledge. In the past this specialist knowledge has been limited to managers and engineers in the quality department. Juran insists on a break with tradition and the devising of a quality programme to involve every employee.

This training programme heavily emphasizes the importance of the customer, whether internal or external, or indeed the end user. He illustrates this idea through his 'quality spiral'.

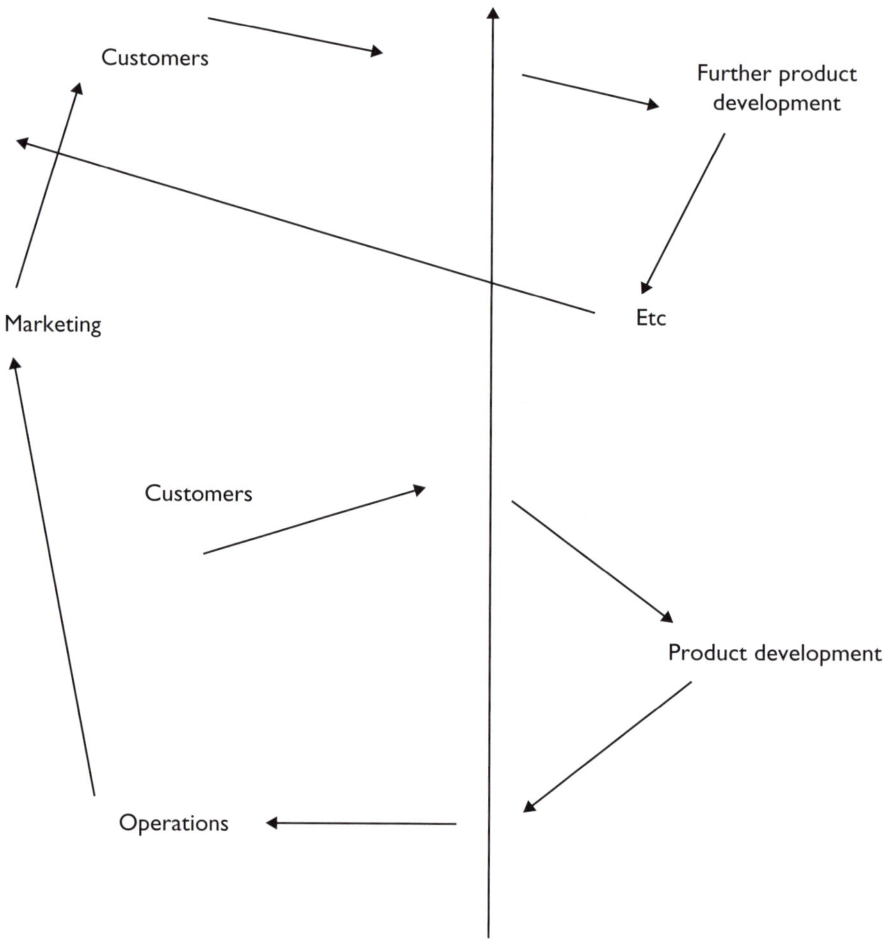

Figure A2 Juran's 'quality spiral'

The parameters affecting the external customer must be based on meeting competition in the marketplace, while those affecting the internal customer are based on getting rid of internal waste. The quality programme should incorporate statistical process control techniques within its training remit.

It is apparent that a high percentage of quality improvement programmes fail to achieve their full potential or simply fail altogether. Tom Peters says that 98 per cent of all such programmes fail. Juran suggests that this is due to:

- no detailed identification tasks
- no hierarchy of responsibility
- no structured process of 'how' to tackle the tasks
- no suitable management performance review.

However, Juran does present his formula for results as follows:

- establish specific goals
- establish plans to reach these goals
- assign clear responsibility for meeting goals
- assign rewards on results achieved.

There are no short cuts to quality, and Juran insists that the majority of problems are the fault of poor management rather than poor workmanship.

Philip B. Crosby

Crosby is best known for developing the programme known as 'zero defects' and his belief that 'quality is free'. He suggests that the things which cost an organization money are all the things that prevent jobs being done right the first time. So when the proper corrective action is taken, these cost areas may be removed.

Crosby proposes five absolutes of quality management:

1. Quality should be developed as conforming to requirements, not as 'goodness' or 'elegance'
2. The system for causing quality is prevention not detection
3. The performance standard must be zero defects
4. The measurement of quality is the price of not conforming
5. There is no such thing as a quality problem.

These absolutes are the basis of his 14-step **quality improvement process** which tackles the following areas:

1. Management commitment
2. Quality improvement teams
3. Quality measurement
4. Cost of quality
5. Quality awareness
6. Corrective action
7. Ad hoc committee for the zero defects programme
8. Supervisor/employee training
9. Zero defects day
10. Goal setting
11. Error cause removal
12. Recognition
13. Quality councils
14. Do it all over again.

Crosby suggests that his zero defects policy is based on the presumption that mistakes are caused in two ways:

- lack of knowledge
- lack of attention.

The first problem is relatively easily tackled by provision of an adequate on-going training programme. However, Crosby sees the second problem as being caused by an attitude problem. This attitude can be changed only by the individual and Crosby recognizes that if the individual makes the changes then he/she is more likely to be committed to that change.

Critics of Crosby imply that his 14-step approach lacks practicality and also that his absolutes ignore the concept of continuous improvement. Crosby, however, argues that continuous improvement is a requirement that must be established by management and that the performance standard would involve all employees constantly improving their work processes.

This requirement suggests that TQM has implications for all aspects of organizational culture (this is discussed in Chapter 1 in more detail).

The implementation of TQM must be designed to fit the organizational culture.

Kaoru Ishikawa

As with other Japanese quality gurus, Ishikawa has paid specific attention to making statistical techniques available to industry. Essentially, his work has emphasized good data collection techniques and also suitable presentation methods. His use of Pareto charts and the development of the Ishikawa or fishbone (cause and effect) diagram as an analytic tool brought him to the fore of Japan's quality drive in the 1950s and 1960s.

Ishikawa is associated with **company-wide quality control** whereby quality is characterized by company-wide participation from top management through everyone in the organization tree. Importantly, everyone in the company should study statistical methods.

Ishikawa stresses that the word 'quality' does not apply simply to the product but to every aspect of the business; for example, design, engineering, research, finance, sales, marketing, the company itself and the human beings. Bearing these ideas in mind the Ishikawa approach results in:

1. Reduced defects
2. Improved reliability
3. Reduced costs
4. Increased production
5. Reduction of wasteful work
6. Improved techniques
7. Reduced inspection and testing costs
8. Rationalized contracts between the vendor and vendee
9. Enlarged sales market
10. Better interdepartmental relationships
11. Reduction of false data and reports
12. More democratic discussions
13. Smoother meetings
14. Better repairs and installation of equipment
15. Better human relations.

QUALITY CIRCLES

One aspect of Ishikawa's company-wide quality control is the practice of quality circles. These circles constitute a voluntary group of around six to eight people from the same work area. The group meets regularly and is led by a supervisor or a team member. The aims of the quality circle are as follows:

- To make improvements and help develop the organization
- To respect human relations and create a good team atmosphere
- To use the normally untapped human potential to the full.

Each person on the team, as already suggested, is introduced to, and trained in, statistical techniques like those listed below:

- Pareto charts
- Cause and effect diagrams
- Stratification
- Check sheets
- Histograms
- Scatter diagrams
- Control charts.

Summary

In summary, all of the quality gurus are aiming for the same ideal, that is, 'perfection'. It is their path to perfection which differs.

While perfection is the aim, they all realize that it is never attainable. What is important is that each person within the organization strives towards making continuous improvements.

All regard management commitment as a fundamental prerequisite to starting a quality improvement programme. Once, and only when this commitment has been gained, should training of the workforce take place.

Differences do appear in the style, content and extent of training from guru to guru. However, all agree that it should involve every employee of the organization and that the training must form part of a life-long programme.

Information toolbox

Quality

Beckford, J. (2002) *Quality a Critical Introduction*, Routledge

Bank, J. (2000) *The Essence of Quality Management*, Financial Times Prentice Hall

Bell, D., McBride, P. and Wilson, G. (1994) *Managing Quality*, Institute of Management Foundation/Butterworth-Heinemann

Crosby, P. (1972) *Quality Is Free*, McGraw-Hill

Crosby, P. (1989) *Let's Talk Quality*, McGraw-Hill

Deming, W.E. (2000) *Out of the Crisis*, Massachusetts Institute of Technology

Department of Trade and Industry (1990) *The Quality Gurus*, HMSO

Gitlow, H. and Oppenheim, A. (1989) *Tools and Methods for the Improvement of Quality*, Irwin Press

Hagan, J.T. (1986) *Principles of Quality Costs*, American Society for Quality Control

Harrington, H.J. (1987) *The Improvement Process: How America's Leading Companies Improve Quality*, McGraw-Hill.

Harrington, H.J. (1991) *Business Process Improvement*, McGraw-Hill

'The Race to Quality Improvement', suppl., (1989) *Fortune*

Macdonald, J. (1998) *Understanding Total Quality Management in a Week*, Hodder and Stoughton/Institute of Management

The EFQM Excellence Model web site www.efqm.org offers free information resources, open and informal discussion programmes and helpful links.

Managing change

Baum, D. (2000) *Lighting in a Bottle: Proven Lessons for Leading Change*, Dearborn Trade Publishing

Bourne, M. and Bourne Pippa (2002) *Change Management in a Week*, CMI & Hodder and Stoughton

Change Management and Managing Best Practice (2002) Industrial Society

Blair, G. and Meadows, S. (1996) *Winning at Change*, Institute of Management Foundation/Pitman Publishing

Chartered Management Institute Checklist 040, *Implementing an Effective Change Programme* and checklist 038 *Mapping an Effective Change Programme*, Checklists can be purchased from Lavis Marketing, Tel. 01865 767575; a discount is available for Institute members

Health and Safety

Stranks, Jeremy (2003) *A Managers Guide to Health and Safety*, Kogan Page

Chartered Management Institute Checklist 157, *Health and Safety Managing the Process* and checklist 056 *Health and Safety Undertaking a Risk Assessment*, Checklists can be purchased from Lavis Marketing, Tel. 01865 767575; a discount is available for Institute members

Hawkins, L. (ed) (2002) *Tolleys Guide to Managing Employee Health*. Butterworths Tolley

Wenham, D. (ed) (2003) *Tolleys Office Health and Safety Handbook*. Butterworths Tolley

The Health and Safety Executive's corporate web site, www.hse.gov.uk, delivers information that ranges from broad health and safety strategy, operational activities, advisory committees and inspection priorities, to campaigns, enforcement and prosecution data and statistics. The site also provides extensive access to free publications.